D0275536

My Name Is Selma

www.penguin.co.uk

My Name Is Selma

The remarkable memoir of a Jewish Resistance
fighter and Ravensbrück survivor

SELMA VAN DE PERRE

Translated by Alice Tetley-Paul and Anna Asbury

BANTAM PRESS

TRANSWORLD PUBLISHERS
Penguin Random House, One Embassy Gardens,
8 Viaduct Gardens, London SW11 7BW
www.penguin.co.uk

Transworld is part of the Penguin Random House group of companies
whose addresses can be found at global.penguinrandomhouse.com

Penguin
Random House
UK

Originally published in Dutch as *Mijn naam is Selma*, 2020.
First published in Great Britain in 2020 by Bantam Press
an imprint of Transworld Publishers

Copyright © Selma van de Perre 2020
English translation copyright © Alice Tetley-Paul and Anna Asbury 2020
Photographs courtesy of the author

Selma van de Perre has asserted her right under the Copyright,
Designs and Patents Act 1988 to be identified as the author of this work.

This publication has been made possible with financial support from the
Dutch Foundation for Literature.

Every effort has been made to obtain the necessary permissions with
reference to copyright material, both illustrative and quoted. We apologize
for any omissions in this respect and will be pleased to make the
appropriate acknowledgements in any future edition.

A CIP catalogue record for this book
is available from the British Library.

ISBNs 9781787633988 (hb)
9781787633995 (tpb)

Typeset in 11.5/15pt Minion Pro by Jouve (UK), Milton Keynes
Printed and bound in Great Britain by Clays Ltd, Elcograf S.p.A.

Penguin Random House is committed to a sustainable
future for our business, our readers and our planet. This book
is made from Forest Stewardship Council® certified paper.

For my parents and sister

Contents

Prologue

6 September 1944 [to Greet Brinkhuis]

Dear Gretchen,
I'm in a cattle wagon with twelve people, in Vught.
Probably headed for Sachsenhausen or Ravensbrück. You
keep your spirits up. I'll do the same, although I do wish
the end was in sight. I'll throw this note out of the train
through a crack in the wall. Bye, my darling.
Kisses, Marga

We were ordered to pack up our toothbrushes and other belongings and wait outside. It was clear we were to be taken somewhere else, but where? We didn't know. I thought it would be safer to stay at Camp Vught than to go off into the unknown, so I decided to hide under a mattress. I let the other women go ahead and stayed behind in the barracks, but I wasn't quick enough. The SS guard – the *Aufseherin* – turned up while I was still only half hidden. She ordered me to hurry up, dragged me outside by my arm and pushed me into the final wagon. This slight delay worked to my advantage: there weren't many women inside that one yet. The others were packed, and the poor women inside – including my friends from the camp – spent the next three days travelling in terrible conditions.

There were only twelve or so women in my wagon. I didn't know any of them. Some of them were younger – in their twenties, like me. They weren't political prisoners, as I was, but 'asocials', who'd done something the Germans didn't like. They realized I was different – educated, and so on. Most of them turned out to be prostitutes who had been rounded up to be treated for sexually transmitted diseases.

In the camp they'd worked in the kitchen, and had managed to sneak a big box of bread and sausage on board, as well as a barrel of soup. This was a huge stroke of luck; I knew the other wagons wouldn't have any such supplies. But, as they began to bicker over the food – some of them wanted to start on it straight away – I realized these women clearly didn't appreciate their good fortune.

We assumed we were on our way to somewhere in Germany, but seeing as we didn't know how long the journey would take I thought it would be sensible to ration the provisions. I put this to the other women cautiously, and luckily they listened. They asked me to hand out the food, and I was honoured to do so. I ladled the soup into portions, and sliced the bread and sausage – they could see I was doing my best to give everyone an equal share.

There was sufficient space for all of us to sit down on the floor of the wagon, and some of us had a bit of wall to lean against as well. There wasn't much conversation between us. The kitchen girls talked together a bit – they knew one another already. As time passed they became a little friendlier towards me – they shared some supplies of toilet paper, for instance. And on that paper I hastily scribbled a note to my good friend in Amsterdam, Greet Brinkhuis.

I told her I was on a train that was probably heading for Germany. When we stopped at the first station – the last town in the Netherlands before we did indeed pass into Germany – I pushed the note through a gap between the wooden planks of the wagon's wall. Even though it was very unlikely that the message would ever reach her, it was worth a try.

The journey seemed interminable, even for those of us in that privileged final wagon. I was feeling anxious, but there was also a sense that the war wouldn't last much longer. We knew that the Allies were already at the border. I knew that I couldn't do anything to change what was happening, so I tried not to worry about it too much. There was simply no point.

We slept on the bare wooden floor of the wagon. It was uncomfortable, but it must have been far worse for my friends in the other wagons – with fifty or sixty people packed inside they wouldn't even have been able to sit down. And they wouldn't have had any food. Although I didn't realize it at the time, I was lucky.

After three days and two nights locked up in the wagons, we reached our destination on 8 September. The sliding doors of the cattle wagon opened and we caught our first glimpse of what we later found out was Ravensbrück. Ironically, this grim and terrible place is located by a large lake – the Schwedtsee – in beautiful surroundings, but we couldn't see anything of that. The SS officers waiting for us on the platform had large dogs with them and were brandishing whips. The dogs were barking and the men, as well as the female guards – the *Aufseherinnen* – were yelling at us to get out of the wagon.

'*Schnell, schnell, schnell! Heraus, heraus, heraus!*'

Quick, quick, quick! Out, out, out!

We were terrified.

1

The Artist and the Milliner: *My family*

I'm sitting here in my quiet house in London and looking at a photo taken in 1940. It's of my mother, younger sister and me. We're relaxing in Aunt Sara's garden in Amsterdam, which, at that moment, was still a peaceful spot. My mother, whom we fondly called Mams, was fifty-one at the time, my sister Clara twelve, and I was eighteen. It's an everyday snapshot of an ordinary family; we were having a pleasant afternoon, enjoying the garden and one another's company. A model image of family time: loving, secure, comfortable, predictable. There's no hint in our faces of what was to come in the following three years: the deaths of my father, mother and Clara; my grandma; Aunt Sara, her husband Arie and their two sons; and so many other family members.

None of these deaths were due to natural causes or accidents. They were the result of the atrocities that were already spreading across Europe when the photo was taken, and which would soon infiltrate the Netherlands. Before those catastrophic events, we hadn't comprehended what a privilege it was to lead an anonymous life. I can still hardly believe that people who should have remained unremarkable ended up memorialized on lists and monuments – because they had fallen victim to the most systemic mass murder the world has ever known.

Like most people, I was born into an ordinary family whose experiences were noteworthy only to those involved. My grandpa on my father's side, Levi Velleman, was an antiques dealer in Schagen. He ran a shop there and another in Haarlem, but he was never a wealthy man. My grandma on my father's side, Saartje Velleman (née Slagter), was a housewife, like most women in her day – although she didn't quite conform to the stereotype as she wasn't all that good at it. She was a hopeless cook and cleaner, and her eldest daughter, my aunt Greta, told me that the house was always a mess, with clothes thrown haphazardly into drawers, so that no one could find anything. There was a live-in maid who did all the heavy work, but as Aunt Greta grew up she took on more and more responsibility for the general household tasks and cared for her younger brothers and sisters.

My father, Barend Levi Velleman, first child of Levi and Saartje, was born on 10 April 1889. His successful birth was likely a relief to my grandpa, whose first wife – Betje – had died in childbirth, followed four days later by their baby boy, also named Barend. The Vellemans named the firstborn son of each generation Barend Levi and Levi Barend by turns, because they were descended from the biblical tribe of Levi.

Grandpa Velleman must have been very keen to start a family, because on 20 June 1888, just four months after the death of his first wife, he married Grandma. Saartje, five and a half years his senior, was thirty when my father was born – in those days that was considered old to be having a first child. But Saartje was a strong woman: she bore ten children in total, the last when she was forty-three. She survived my grandpa, who died in 1923 at the age of fifty-eight, by many years. Who knows what great age she might have reached had she not been murdered in Auschwitz, aged eighty-three, on 28 September 1942, just a couple of weeks before my father, her son, was also killed.

The arrival of a healthy son was cause for celebration. But even completely normal families experience trauma, and for my father the feeling of being cherished soon disappeared. On 16 April 1892, when he was three years old, his sister Greta was born. One day, when Saartje was changing Greta's nappy, there was a knock on the door. Saartje went to answer it, leaving little Barend behind with the baby. When she returned, Greta was on the floor crying. Saartje blamed my father and assumed he'd pushed his little sister off the table in a fit of jealousy. Aunt Greta later said she'd probably just rolled off, but perhaps Grandma was right. As with so many family tales, we'll never know the truth. In any case, my father was sent to stay with his paternal grandparents. He spent the rest of his childhood living with them in Alkmaar, where he grew up more or less as their son.

It's hard to comprehend how Grandma was able to give up her firstborn, but within three months of Greta's birth she was pregnant again, so perhaps caring for a toddler as well as a baby while carrying another was too much for her. Organizing a household wasn't her forte in the first place and it must have been a relief to have a few of her responsibilities taken over. My father's grandparents were, in any case, very pleased to have him live with them.

As the family continued to grow, my father remained in Alkmaar while his parents and seven surviving younger brothers and sisters stayed together. Being the only one excluded from the family made him feel terribly rejected. His early exile dogged him for the rest of his life; he never forgave his mother for not taking him back. Although he did have contact with her during his childhood, as an adult he refused to talk to her for years.

I never met his family until I was in my late teens, with the exception of Uncle Harry, one of Pa's younger brothers with whom he kept in touch. I assume he occasionally heard word from his other siblings, although he never mentioned it. I was curious about them, but the estrangement was such a part of our family life that I took it all for granted and barely gave it a second thought.

In 1941, when I was nineteen, this situation came to an end. One day the doorbell rang and I answered. On the door-step stood an elegant woman dressed in black, her hair piled up high on her head.

'Is your father at home?' she asked.

I fetched Pa.

'Mother!' he cried.

I looked on in astonishment.

I was really glad to meet new family members and to get to know Aunt Greta especially, since everyone had always said I resembled her, in both appearance and behaviour. At first I had taken the comparison as an insult, knowing that my father held a grudge against her, but she turned out to be a lovely woman. She ended up surviving the war because she was married to a Christian, and it was a pleasure to visit her after the liberation.

Grandma asked Pa if I could go with her to visit one of her other granddaughters, my cousin Sarah, who had been placed in a well-known children's home outside Amsterdam. We made the journey together by train, and Sarah and I became great friends. It was really lovely to have more family around me. The opportunity to restore the relationship with my father's family was very important to us. Love makes life worth living, and I believe Grandma was trying to make amends before it was too late.

Tragically, the small steps we'd made towards healing the rift came to an abrupt end before we'd achieved much more than a rapprochement. In 1942, Grandma – who still lived independently in Haarlem – was forced to move to a Jewish nursing home in Amsterdam. Mams, Clara and I went to visit her every week, but later that year all residents of the home were sent to Westerbork transit camp. From there, they were transported to Auschwitz and murdered.

The nursing home was simply stripped bare. At the time we didn't know that it had happened, and weren't able to say goodbye to her. Grandma had disappeared. I don't know exactly when she was transported, but it was probably only shortly before she died. At that point there was so much confusion among the Jewish community that it was difficult to keep track of where everyone was, even close family members. Only after the war did I discover her fate. One of Pa's younger brothers had said she'd died in Westerbork, but when I consulted the lists I saw that she had been murdered at Auschwitz on 28 September 1942.

My great-grandfather had a factory where the rag-and-bone men brought their rags to be made into paper. Business was going well and Pa was reaping the benefits of his grandfather's relative prosperity. He was a clever boy who had skipped a number of years in school, and the family had high expectations of him. He attended a state secondary school until, at the age of seventeen, he was sent to a yeshiva (a Talmudical school) in Amsterdam. His grandparents were devout people and had set their hearts on a religious career for him. He had a good tenor voice and they wanted him to become a cantor or a rabbi.

But Pa had very different ideas – it had long been his ambition to go into theatre. In his teens he had directed plays that were performed by friends and relatives – not just at parties to entertain the family, but also at community events. I remember a review in the local newspaper, which contained phrases such as 'outstanding job by the young Barend Velleman'. He was utterly passionate about it and showed real talent.

Always a rebellious boy, he renounced the faith that played such a major role in his grandparents' life. At the yeshiva he questioned his teachers repeatedly on religious issues. They despaired of him because he wasn't sufficiently obedient to Jewish doctrine. He clearly wasn't cut out to be a rabbi. Twice he was sent home, and on both occasions his grandfather beat him but took him back to the school.

Then Pa took matters into his own hands and used his pocket money to buy a ferry ticket to England. My great-grandfather went to the police and asked them to bring his grandson, who was still a minor, back home. Whether or not they actually got involved, one way or another Pa was indeed compelled to return home. After that, my great-grandparents realized that they were wasting their time and money by expecting Pa to pursue a religious vocation.

Pa immediately entered the theatre, where he worked under the name Ben Velmon, and from then on he earned his keep in the entertainment industry. He performed as an actor, singer and variety-show presenter.

During the First World War, a million Belgians had fled to the Netherlands, where they stayed in camps. After the conflict they returned to their villages and towns, which had been largely destroyed, but while the Belgian refugees were in the Dutch camps, Pa organized entertainment for them. A number of young singers and comedians among them, whom he'd employed and encouraged, went on to become famous. To show their gratitude the refugees melted down some of their gold and had a beautiful signet ring made and inscribed with my father's initials. Regrettably the ring disappeared during the Second World War.

It was an exciting life, but very insecure, entailing a nomadic existence for our family. We moved house frequently because of fluctuations in his income – sometimes living in abject poverty and sometimes in relative prosperity – but Pa did the thing he loved and I was very proud of him.

*

My mother's full name was Femmetje, but no one in the family called her that. She was always known as Fem. She was born on 10 August 1889 in Alkmaar, the daughter of David and Clara Spier. The middle child of seven, she had three sisters and three brothers. Grandpa had a large clothing and haberdashery shop in Alkmaar, and later opened one in Den Helder as well.

My mother's parents met up regularly with Pa's grandparents in Alkmaar to play cards. Pa was a good card player and often joined in, while my mother poured the tea. That's how they got to know each other. When Pa was sent to the yeshiva in Amsterdam, Mams was determined to follow him and came up with a clever ruse.

She asked her parents if she could train to become a milliner. Friends of her parents had a shop in Amsterdam where they made magnificent fashionable hats, and Mams became their apprentice. With a background in fashion and haberdashery it's not surprising she opted for hat-making, although women in the Spier family were never permitted to pursue a real commercial career; they only made hats and clothes for the family, alongside carrying out their day-to-day household tasks. Of course, the real reason for her departure to Amsterdam was my father. He visited her regularly in the house where she stayed, and when he left the yeshiva they married in Alkmaar, on 21 March 1911.

On 29 December 1911, their first child was born: my eldest brother, Louis. His official name was Levi Barend – like my father's father – but we always called him Louis. Two years later, on 26 December 1913, my brother David arrived. My father had become successful in the meantime, performing in many of the biggest theatres in the Netherlands, and he, Mams and my brothers lived in an elegant house at 445 Prinsengracht. Into this family and these prosperous conditions, on 7 June 1922 a little girl was born at the Wilhelmina Gasthuis hospital. That was me: Selma Velleman.

2

Jumping Over Ditches: *My childhood*

When I was born, Pa was on tour in Europe and decided to move the family to Zandvoort in the north of the Netherlands, to be near the sea, where the air was cleaner than in Amsterdam, mainly for the sake of the children. It was already one of the foremost spa resorts in the country.

We moved there when I was two weeks old and stayed until I was four years old. Of course, I don't remember much of that time, but I do know my brother David would often drag me over the sand in a handcart when I was about a year old, as the family had photos of this. Sadly, like so many other things, those pictures disappeared during the war.

In 1926 we moved to Alkmaar. My father's European tour was over by then and he was probably out of work. It might seem like an uncertain existence for a young family, but I benefited from it when the war put an end to any form of stability. I wasn't ever someone who became attached to a specific place or who struggled to adjust to change, and I'm sure that helped me deal with the terrifying, unpredictable events that were to unfold.

Our house in Alkmaar was a magnificent end terrace, surrounded by meadows and a ditch. Several other children lived in the street and we all enjoyed playing outside. One day the older children were jumping the ditch, and although I was only four I wanted to try it too; I was always a daring child. Of course I was too small to bridge the gap and fell into the water. The other children made such a racket that the barber on the corner came rushing over and fished me out with a long pole. In those innocent, peaceful times a minor incident such as that caused a great stir. People were talking and laughing about it for days. I also remember the joy I felt as a little girl when my friends and I would run to the cheese market after school, and the dealers with their large, round wheels of cheese. With a long, pointed cheese trier they would draw out a sample and break off small pieces for us to taste.

Every Sunday we would visit my great-grandmother in the house where my father had lived until he got married. I was only very young, so can hardly remember anything about her, but I can still see her sitting at the end of a long table with a big coffee pot over a little candle. Her clothes were always black and she wore a lace cap tied under her chin. My parents would talk to her while the housekeeper, Roos Meyboom, whom we called Aunt Roos, took me to the kitchen for a piece of cake or some sweets.

Aunt Roos was a loyal housekeeper and always took very good care of my great-grandparents. She was particularly fond of Pa, whom she had more or less raised herself. When my great-grandmother died on 12 December 1926, Aunt Roos came to live with us as my nanny. Her bedroom was next to mine, and every morning I would creep into bed with her and she would tell me stories while the rest of the house was sleeping.

One morning I went to Aunt Roos' room as usual and saw

that a chair had been placed in front of her door. It seemed strange, but I simply pushed it out of the way and climbed into bed with her as usual. As soon as I crept under the covers I was overcome with confusion; the bed that was normally so lovely and warm was now cold, as was Aunt Roos. I couldn't understand why she wouldn't talk to me, however much I begged for a story.

When my mother came to fetch me and I told her Aunt Roos was cold, she explained that Roos had died in the night. They had placed the chair in front of the door to try to stop me from going in. I'm not sure exactly of the year this happened, but it was probably around 1927, when I was five. It was my first encounter with death.

Nineteen twenty-seven was also the year in which we left our magnificent house in Alkmaar and moved to an apartment above a large café in the centre of the town. It was clearly a step down, so there can't have been much money coming in at that point.

One day my mother's younger sister, Aunt Suze, came to visit. As we were strolling around the town, we passed a shop with a beautiful children's chair in the window. It was round and made of wicker. It was love at first sight. I wanted it so much, but my mother said that would be impossible. My aunt replied that she would buy it for me and my mother protested. Aunt Suze took no notice, walked into the shop and bought it. I was overjoyed. It was quite a gift for a child whose parents could no longer afford much. I loved to sit in that little chair and cherished it for a long time.

Although we had no contact with Pa's family, we saw Mams'

brothers and sisters frequently and I was very close to them. Of course, Aunt Suze was my favourite after her gift of the chair! Tragically, she died only two years later of peritonitis that had been misdiagnosed as period pain. She was married to Jacques Limburg, a friend and theatre colleague of my father's, and she left behind a son, Loutje, who was just six years old.

After Suze's death, Uncle Jacques was persuaded to move Loutje to Leiden, to live with my mother's brother, Joop, and his wife, Jet. They would be able to offer him a better life than a widower could, it was felt, and they were very keen to care for him.

In the end, for some reason or other, Uncle Joop and Aunt Jet didn't keep Loutje with them, and he was placed in a children's home where they were governors. I'm not sure why: perhaps he wasn't able to settle down with them, having lost his mother and been taken away from his father, or perhaps they thought he would be better off around other children. I couldn't imagine being separated from my parents.

In 1928, just after New Year, it was time for us to move again – back to Amsterdam. This time we lived in real poverty. We weren't eligible for benefits because you could only claim if you had lived in Amsterdam for a year, and we had been away. We weren't able to make use of the help offered by the synagogue either, because we weren't religious.

Our first flat in the city was on Ambonstraat in the east of the city, but we couldn't keep up with the rent and had to leave. Mams was heavily pregnant at the time, so an artist friend took us in. He had children himself, which meant there was no space for my father and brothers, who stayed near by with another friend from the theatre.

On 3 April 1928, while we were staying with our friends, my little sister Clara was born in hospital. Fortunately, Pa soon managed to find a flat in a Jewish neighbourhood, so we ended up living with them for only a week. Mams told me Pa had said we were a family and should live together whatever happened, which showed his longing for a loving family life after his own experiences.

Every Monday at my primary school the children were supposed to pay tuition fees, but we weren't able to because we were so poor. Each week I would go in and say I'd forgotten the money. Each week I would have to stand in the corner as a punishment. I'll never forget the injustice. The teachers must have known what was really going on; it happened week after week. Although I admit it must have been hard for others to understand how poor we really were, as I was always very well dressed. My aunt from Leiden would send us clothes when her daughter Klaartje, who was five or six years older than me, grew out of them. Mams did a wonderful job of altering them and I even remember a teacher saying to me, 'What, another new coat already?'

So, from afar, people probably thought we were relatively well off. Our neighbour knew how poor we were, though, because one day she very kindly gave us a banana, which my mother mashed up for Clara. I looked at it longingly and was given a teaspoonful. What a treat!

Living in such poverty took a toll on my health and the following year, when I was seven, I woke one day with a high fever.

I began to scream, then collapsed. My parents called the doctor, who diagnosed pneumonia and pleurisy – inflammation of the membranes of the chest cavity – which was causing fluid to build up in and around my lungs. Dr Antonie Menco – I'll never forget his name – decided to operate immediately and remove the pus from my chest. He appointed my father as his assistant. Pa had to stand close by and spray liquid from a syringe onto my back while the doctor inserted a needle to withdraw the fluid. The spray felt like ice-cold water, but now I understand that it must have been a local anaesthetic. Mams was instructed to hold me firmly to prevent me from moving.

While the doctor was carrying out the procedure, my eldest brother Louis came home singing and whistling as usual. 'Close the door and stop that racket,' Dr Menco shouted out. 'Do you want your sister to die?'

Poor Louis had no idea what was happening, but he obeyed.

My father always said that Dr Menco saved my life. He sent him a large box of cigars to thank him. I ended up going to the same secondary school as Dr Menco's daughter, and it was a great pleasure to tell her the story of her father's skilful treatment.

I was ill for a long time after that. Our flat was chilly and damp, which of course didn't help. When I had rallied somewhat, I was sent to a sanatorium in Laren in 't Gooi, southeast of Amsterdam, where the air was better than in the centre of the city. They thought I might have tuberculosis. My cousin, David Roet, was there for the same reason, in the men's wing. Every day the patients were wheeled out onto the veranda, bed and all – even in winter when it was freezing and snowy. The veranda ran the length of the sanatorium, and the children's beds were placed on the left, the adults' on the right.

One day, my father brought six magnificent strawberries for me, packaged in a padded box. Strawberries were rarely imported in winter, so if you could find them at all then they cost a fortune. I knew they were a very special treat and they looked absolutely delicious. Clearly Pa was earning good money again, and this was his way of demonstrating his love and cheering me up.

On his next visit, he asked me if I'd enjoyed them, and I had to admit I hadn't been allowed to eat them. Pa was furious and went to the matron to demand an explanation. She told him patients weren't allowed to keep their own fruit or sweets – the sanatorium's policy was to collect everything that was brought in and to share it out. Of course, six strawberries couldn't be properly shared out, so I suspect a member of staff ate them.

Another time, Pa brought a large bunch of beautiful bananas, one of which I hid before the rest were collected. I took it to the toilet to eat. Sadly, one of the nurses walked past and caught me. She pressed her big, heavy knuckles into my shoulder, precisely in the spot where I'd been treated for pleurisy. Even now, more than ninety years later, it still hurts when I catch a cold or accidentally knock myself there.

Although I was very young, I understood that such gifts were pointless. I told my family not to bring any more fruit, but still they kept on doing it. I don't think they could bring themselves to turn up empty-handed. One of my uncles brought me a really lovely paint set, but I wasn't allowed to use it. The staff were probably afraid the bed sheets and covers would get dirty.

It was a terribly strict regime, and when I look back on how children were treated in those days it strikes me as horrifying. Once, a girl got out of bed without permission. From then on, all the children were forced to wear a jacket with long strings that were tied under the bed. We could hardly move. I was so restricted in my movements that if anyone came to visit, I could barely even kiss them. I felt completely humiliated. You could call this my first experience of imprisonment, and perhaps it toughened me up and helped to prepare me for what my future held.

I was supposed to spend a year in that dreadful place, but in the end I was permitted to return home after about eight months. While I was there Pa had indeed prospered and we were able to afford a nurse, making it safe for me to go home. When I left the sanatorium, Pa, in one of his trademark gestures of generosity, treated all the patients to a *jodenkoek* – traditional Jewish shortbread biscuits – which were sold in tins with a yellow label. He made sure to send lots of tins so that every patient would receive a biscuit.

While I was away our family had moved to a lovely house in Diemen, which had a bathroom and a garden, and it wasn't as damp as the old flat. It was magnificent. Pa was doing well financially because he was managing one of the first Luna Parks in the Netherlands, which had opened in Diemen in the summer of 1931. The original Luna Park had opened in 1903 in Coney Island, Brooklyn, New York, offering funfair-style attractions and shows, and was followed by outposts in

America and Europe. The park was a great success; newspaper photos show lines and lines of people queuing to enter.

There was a permanent circus at the park as well as a riding school where I learned to ride. I loved it. A group of dwarves we called the 'Lilliputian family' also performed there; I remember their father coming round to apply for a job. There were concerts and plays, dozens of game stalls and an ice rink. The owner of the Italian ice-cream stall said we could drop by any time for a free ice cream. We were all partial to a sweet treat, so after dinner Pa often sent me there to fetch a large bowlful.

For a while life was wonderful, but our prosperity was short lived. The American stock market crash in 1929 threw countries across the globe into a deep crisis, including the Netherlands. Business went downhill. People no longer spent money on frivolities such as ice rinks and fairs when they could skate for free on the canals and rivers, and they no longer had money for leisure activities such as horse riding. Luna Park was forced to shut its doors.

My father tried to get work in artistic circles and on stage again, but that had more or less dried up too. He began to drink heavily and regularly came home drunk. It's still a mystery to me how he always got back safely from Amsterdam to Diemen. 'God must have special guardian angels watching over him,' my mother always said.

He hoped there would be more employment opportunities in the city, so we moved back to Amsterdam, into a maisonette occupying the third and fourth floors of a property on Tweede Jan van der Heijdenstraat. The day we moved in, the girl who lived opposite at number 44 looked through her window on the third floor and saw me in the street below, trying to play alone. She came down and said, 'Would you like to play with my ball?'

And that was that. Greet Brinkhuis and I became the best of friends. I was skinny, dark-haired and from a large Jewish family. She was a big blonde Dutch girl, the only child of strict Catholic parents. Her father was a book binder and helped at the church around the corner. The family went to church every morning and prayed before and after every meal. Greet loved coming round to our house to join in with family life. She was one of the most loyal friends you could wish for and we've remained close all our lives.

All the bedrooms in our new home had a wash basin, which was unusual at the time, and there was even a bathroom too. There were also gymnastic rings and a swing attached to the top-storey ceiling for the children, so my friends loved coming round to play. The house had a flat roof, and Louis and I would climb out of a spare-room window to sunbathe on it. I remember we saw a zeppelin fly overhead one day, and we watched from our spot on the rooftop, breathless.

Life was good. We loved the apartment. I remember the spacious sitting room with three windows and a large folding table in particular. I had been given a ping-pong set and we used the table to play on. It was unusual to have space for such games, and our cousins and friends were always excited to visit. Louis tried to exclude me – I think he found it irritating having a younger sister who couldn't play as well as him – but

Pa would stand up for me. 'It's her game,' he would say. 'Let her join in!'

No wonder I adored him so; he was always a wonderful father to me.

We lived on Tweede Jan van der Heijdenstraat for several years, but the stairs were so steep that my parents grew tired of it. In 1936 we moved to an apartment in Jan Lievenstraat, also in the neighbourhood of De Pijp. One of my father's cousins owned a huge furniture shop, Dick & Co., and Pa bought all our furniture new from him when we moved, so we must have been reasonably well off at that time. Before that we had only ever had antique furniture, so it was an exciting change. Pa also dropped in on one of his brothers, who ran two antique shops in Haarlem, and came back with a desk for me and a beautiful oil painting for the house.

'They owe me that after everything they did to me,' Pa said, meaning that his family hadn't given him any share of the inheritance when my grandpa died in 1923. His brother was already working in their father's shop at the time and took it over after his death. But perhaps Pa was also referring to his exile from the family when he was little. I don't know if he got the items for free or at a discounted price; in those days, parents didn't discuss such things with their children.

Our new interior marked a fresh, optimistic start and we stayed in Jan Lievenstraat until we were compelled to leave everything behind in 1942.

Despite our family's fluctuating fortunes and the periods of poverty we experienced, I was a very happy child. Pa was a devoted father, determined to cherish and protect his children, and the love of our parents was all that mattered. Not only was I loved, I was also encouraged to develop my talents.

In contrast to most men of his generation, Pa was very liberal. I was lucky to be his daughter and I benefited greatly from his progressive ideas. I remember sitting at the table when one of my brothers told me to fetch him a glass of water. 'No, she won't,' Pa said. 'She's not your maid. Fetch it yourself.'

There was no sense that I was expected to do the housework because I was a girl either. I wasn't permitted to do the washing-up or other household tasks – Pa would always say, 'Selma has to study.' He wanted me to go into science, but the war eventually put an end to my education.

Besides being progressive, Pa was also very well organized. When he wasn't working, he did all the shopping and marked the date on everything he bought – something I still do now. We were very similar and I recognize his influence on me, something I find very comforting. It's been my way of keeping him with me all my life.

That doesn't mean I didn't feel ashamed, though, when I had friends round. Pa wasn't generally all that drunk, but he was often far from sober. I would go to my friend Mary Rudolphus's house regularly, since she lived near school. Her mother invited me to theirs for lunch during the school week, when all the children went home to eat, because otherwise I'd have had to walk half an hour home and then back again. I would also help Mary with her homework because I was very good at maths, and Mary wasn't. I was keen to invite Mary round to ours, but on the occasion I did my father came home tipsy. I was deeply embarrassed and wished the ground would swallow me up.

My mother really struggled with Pa's drinking too. A couple of years before war broke out, she decided enough was enough and left. She went to a friend who lived near by, Jo Nijland. Jo and her husband were what my father called 'artists' fleas' – they weren't artists themselves, but always hung around with them. He disapproved of this, so I think he was furious that Mams went to them of all people. She came back the following day and never left again, but it goes some way towards showing how fed up she was. She almost never made decisions herself, so it was exceptional for her to do such a thing. She must have reached the depths of despair.

I forgave Pa a great deal because I loved him so much. He loved my mother very much too. When he came home drunk he sometimes cried out, 'But I never go with other women. You're the only one I love, Fem!'

My mother was a friendly, mild-mannered woman; her sisters called her 'darling Fem' and she was the sweetest woman in the world. She was very attractive, petite, with dark hair and eyes, and a pale complexion. She had a beautiful figure when she was young. When we arrived home from school she was always there, milk and biscuits at the ready. She would make our clothes or alter items given to us by others, and whenever there was money, she would take us shopping for new clothes. I enjoyed those outings so much.

My little sister Clara was born a couple of months before

my sixth birthday. She was a beautiful baby and a sweet child, with a character as mild as that of our mother, whom she resembled. My brother David also shared Mams' features, whereas Louis and I took after our father, in personality as well.

Since we were the youngest and extremely close, Clara and I always shared a bedroom. One of our favourite games was to play schools. I made little cardboard benches and small cardboard girls to sit at them. I was the teacher and Clara was one of my pupils. Because I was six years older, I think she saw me as a grown-up.

When she was old enough we would walk to school together, and I'd drop her off in the morning and collect her again in the afternoon. The older she grew, the clearer it became that she wasn't academic; she was more interested in household affairs. In 1941, when Jews were prohibited from attending non-Jewish schools, she had to give up her state education and was sent to a Jewish housekeeping school. It suited her well, as she learned sewing and other household skills. She loved to swim too and earned her first certificate for it when she was only three.

I also got on well with my brothers. Of course they teased me, as big brothers do, but David often took care of me when I was very small, and when I was older Louis used to take me to the pictures. Nicely brought-up girls were only permitted to see films such as the Mickey Mouse animations, and I was absolutely banned from watching films intended for adults, but one day Louis took me to see *King Kong*. Pa was furious; after that I wasn't allowed to go to the cinema any more.

So this was my family: my imperfect but loving father, my darling mother, my two brothers and my beautiful, innocent little sister. They're the people with whom I spent my very happy childhood. And three of them were taken away and slaughtered like animals.

3

Second-class Citizens: *The occupation*

In 1936 the Netherlands began to receive immigrants from Germany. They told troubling tales of National Socialism and what happened to people who renounced the Nazis. At first we didn't pay much attention. David even travelled to Austria in 1938, shortly after it had been occupied and annexed by Nazi Germany; a rather provocative act for a young Jewish man, you might say in hindsight.

Everyone thought the Netherlands would remain neutral if war broke out – as it had done in the First World War. As a result, Dutch men were being paid to marry foreign Jewish girls on the assumption that those girls would be awarded Dutch citizenship and therefore be safe. David was twenty-four at the time, and in his youthful impulsiveness such a venture struck him as an exciting thing to do.

He travelled to Austria with a Jewish friend who was also going to marry a Jewish girl – they saw it as a big adventure. He and his friend each received 200 guilders in payment, which was a great deal of money at the time. David's future father-in-law was the wealthy owner of a large factory. Since David was under thirty years of age, he needed Pa's consent for the marriage to go ahead. Pa disapproved of the whole undertaking, but since David no longer lived at home he probably thought him old enough to make his own choices and gave his approval.

None of us ever met David's first bride. After all, it was just a business agreement; the girl never came back with him to live in the Netherlands. When David returned, Pa refused to talk about what had happened and soon the incident faded into insignificance. What it did give us was an impression of the extent to which Jews in other countries felt threatened by the Nazis.

I was a typical Dutch girl in those days. I attended secondary school, learning English, French and German. I very much wanted to make progress in those languages, but I can't claim I knew much about the rest of Europe. People hardly travelled back then, and my parents didn't have much money to spare, so if we went on holiday it was to somewhere in the Netherlands.

I'd never been abroad, but in the summer of 1939 I was given the chance to go on a school trip to England. For a girl of seventeen it was an exciting opportunity! It was also the reason behind a new acquisition in my wardrobe: a blue cardigan, knitted by my mother, with a zip – very modern at the time! I would be immensely grateful for it later on in Ravensbrück, as it was so cold there and we only had thin dresses otherwise. When I wore it in that place, I held close the thought of Mams knitting it and the memory of her wanting me to look good on my first journey abroad.

When my classmates and I left for England, there was a prevailing sense that war might be on the way. One of the girls had been given a large sum of money by her father – in case war did break out and she was unable to return to the Netherlands. I remember her asking me what she should do with it. I advised her to leave it with her host family rather than carry it around London. The idea that war was imminent and we might not be able to get home wasn't something that particularly worried us, though; in fact, I was already looking forward to another school trip to France the following year!

In hindsight, the Dutch might have seemed naive, but even when Britain declared war on Germany at the end of the summer, we barely paid any attention. We did wonder about the effects of the occupation in Poland, Germany and Yugoslavia, but in a general sense in the same way you're interested in international politics. We couldn't imagine that the declaration of war would affect us.

Less than a year later, however, the life we'd taken for granted would come to an abrupt end. The Germans would enter the Netherlands and begin to commit acts so horrific that I now struggle to believe they really happened, in spite of having experienced them myself.

Young Dutch men were conscripted to join the army when they turned eighteen, and from the age of twenty they had to train for a set number of weeks. After his military service, David went to work for Uncle Arie in his clothes shop while continuing to participate in compulsory training. In 1939, when England declared war on Germany, he was called up, aged twenty-five. He ended up in the medical service of what later became known as the Princess Irene Brigade, a Dutch medical unit that was subsequently stationed in the UK after the collapse of the Dutch government in 1940.

Louis hadn't had any military training. He'd always wanted to go to sea and had attended a maritime college, but he was turned away by the Royal Netherlands Navy. They told him his chest was too narrow and he wasn't tall enough, so he went into theatre like Pa. He became an actor and singer, and performed in a number of films, such as *Bleeke Bet* (1934) and *De Jantjes* (1936), which were produced in the Dutch 'Hollywood' – the Cinetone Studio in Amsterdam.

Unlike Pa, however, Louis's dream had never been to perform, and he still longed to go to sea. A couple of months before the war broke out, he bumped into a friend from the maritime college who worked in the merchant navy, and learned that there was a vacancy at the Hollandsche Stoomboot Maatschappij – the Holland Steamship Company. Excited about the opportunity, Louis applied and was successful. The company took him on and he followed their training programme for several months before starting work as an engineer on a ship. So he found himself in the services too, but didn't expect to become involved in the war.

On 10 May 1940, around four o'clock in the morning, Louis woke us all up. I'd been fast asleep and was quite grumpy about being disturbed.

'Wake up! Wake up!' Louis was shouting, as he pulled at my shoulder.

'Go away! Let me sleep!' I grumbled, as I turned over and thought how annoying brothers can be, but he continued tugging at me.

When I heard the rest of the family getting up, I realized

something important must be going on. Reluctantly, I climbed out of my warm bed.

'War!' said Louis. 'We're at war.'

We stared at him in shock, shaking our heads. We couldn't believe our ears. But when we turned on the radio and heard that the German army had crossed the border and there was heavy fighting in progress, we knew it must be true. Germany had invaded the Netherlands, Belgium and Luxembourg without declaring war first. Their plan to take us by surprise had succeeded.

Our entire neighbourhood was awake now, and the news was spreading rapidly. I realized that something extraordinary was happening when Uncle Levi, who was married to my mother's sister Jaan, came over to see us. My father hadn't spoken to him for several years because we hadn't been invited to the wedding of their daughter Zetty. The fact that they now buried the hatchet, and talked as if there had never been bad words between them, was a clear indication that something important was under way.

Louis had to be back on board his ship by six o'clock that morning. Since there was a great deal of confusion about the situation, my father decided to accompany him out of concern for his safety. In the end, Uncle Levi, Clara and I went along too. All public transport was out of service and it took us around an hour to walk to the IJ – the port of Amsterdam. Although there had been all kinds of activity in our neighbourhood, the streets in other districts were as quiet as normal for such an early hour; most people were still asleep and didn't know what was going on.

Four days later the Netherlands surrendered, but at home we were much more concerned about Louis and David's safety than our own. We continued to talk about what might happen to them – their situation seemed much more vulnerable than ours. We kept wondering whether the Germans had got hold of them. The atmosphere in the house was dreadful and we barely slept. Mams even fainted in the kitchen one day, for the first time in her life.

At the end of that month I was due to sit my final school exam. It won't come as a surprise to read that I was so worried about my brothers that I couldn't concentrate on studying. At the start of the exam I was terribly nervous and could hardly bring myself to remain seated in the examination room. I failed. Even in my favourite subject, maths, where I normally achieved high grades, I only received a six – ten being an outstanding mark.

Pa said it would be a good idea to sit the state exam and at least get the certificate. Fortunately I managed to pass that with very good grades. Some people encouraged me to follow in my father's footsteps, but nothing would persuade me to go on stage. 'I want a job with regular hours and a regular wage,' I told Mams.

What I wanted most was to work at the high-end department store De Bijenkorf.

The effects of the German occupation weren't immediately perceptible to us. For a while, life continued more or less as it had before – even for Jewish people. Amsterdam had always been a reasonably tolerant city, and my Jewish identity had never been an issue. My friends weren't Jewish, and my brothers had non-Jewish girlfriends. I didn't have the impression that there was any reason to pay extra attention to that part of my life. Those around me barely mentioned religious differences.

When I celebrated Christmas with my friend Mary Rudolphus, it didn't matter that I was Jewish, even though her father was a devout Christian and very strict when it came to the holiday. We were permitted to read only religious books and sing only religious songs over the period, and we weren't allowed to play games at all. Nevertheless, I was welcomed into their home and liked going there, despite the restrictions. All that mattered was that we were two girls who enjoyed spending time together.

My own family wasn't religious. There were other Jewish girls who didn't attend school on Saturdays because of the Sabbath, but for me it was an ordinary school day. As a result, lots of people didn't realize I was Jewish, including my teachers. Once, the teacher asked for a volunteer to take homework to a Jewish girl who wasn't in class because it was a Jewish holiday, and I offered. The girl's mother gave me some chocolate to say thank you and told me, 'This is special Jewish chocolate, by the way. It's kosher. Perhaps you know what that means.' She had no idea I was Jewish too. At that point it seemed insignificant, but the fact that I didn't look Jewish would later save my life.

Although we weren't practising Jews, our family did identify as Jewish. All three of my siblings learned Hebrew and my brothers also celebrated their bar mitzvahs. Clara had a Torah signed by her teachers, who also invited her to celebrate the Jewish festivals with them, since we didn't do so at home.

It began to dawn on me that our Jewishness now mattered in a way it hadn't before, even though I hadn't been to the synagogue since I was six and hadn't learned any Hebrew. On one of the many trips he made for his entertainment work, Louis had bought me a silver Star of David on a chain. I'd never worn it, but after the occupation I put it on under my clothes. It was an acknowledgement of Jewish affiliation, a sign of solidarity with our fellow Jews. 'Are *you* Jewish?' my gym teacher asked me in astonishment at changing time one day. She'd had no idea.

Bit by bit we heard more rumours about what was happening to Jews in Germany and other occupied countries in Europe. We were terrified, as we didn't know how my brothers were doing. It later transpired that Louis's ship had remained in IJmuiden for five days once the occupation was under way. After that, he travelled all over the world, transporting war supplies. He was lucky not to be torpedoed. After a while we learned that he was at least still alive, as his company, the Hollandsche Stoomboot Maatschappij, started making weekly payments to us that had been deducted from his salary. An HSM employee came round every week to bring us the money – and each time it meant good news to us.

We knew that David and his brigade were stationed in Middelburg, in the southwest of the Netherlands, when the war started. They had engaged in battle there and managed to hold back the Germans for four days. As soon as the Dutch surrendered, David's brigade was ordered to withdraw to Belgium, but shortly afterwards Belgium also surrendered. After that, they were sent to France and eventually to England.

At first, his brigade was stationed in a large Dutch military centre near Wolverhampton, but then David received orders to move to London to become an administrator in the medical division. A good friend of his, who was an officer, went with him and became head of the entire department. Since David had once fallen asleep while on guard during training, he hadn't been promoted and was still a sergeant. Nevertheless, he was appointed head of the secretariat. Although we didn't know it at the time, he was fairly safe there.

The first sign of life we received wasn't until 1942, when Pa got a letter from him via the Red Cross. David had met a young woman in Wolverhampton named Sadie, whom he really wanted to marry. He was therefore asking Pa for certain papers so that he could divorce the Austrian girl he'd married before the war. We had so many worries that this really was the last thing we wanted to deal with. I didn't think he should be pestering Pa with matters of marriage and divorce, and in any case, we had no way of acquiring the papers, as we didn't even know where David's first wife was. I later found out that she'd been sent to Theresienstadt and survived the concentration camp. David never saw her again, though he did succeed in divorcing her after the war. Although we were less than delighted with his request, at least we knew he was safe.

Besides being worried about my brothers, I was preoccupied with finding a job for myself during that first year of war. After I'd taken my exams and finished school, my Jewish background started to restrict my options. Jews were no longer allowed to go to university, so that was ruled out, even if my family had been able to afford it.

Although I'd passed the state examinations, I could no longer apply for government jobs either. The more difficulties I encountered, the more aware I was of this part of my identity. Towards the end of 1940, all Jews working for the state were made redundant. Jewish university lecturers, teachers, doctors and lawyers were permitted to work for Jewish institutions and clinics only from then on. On top of that, Jews and non-Jews were forbidden from entering one another's houses.

'The only person who'll still come round is Greet,' Pa said.

He was right.

In the meantime, I took shorthand and typing courses, and since I'd passed the state examinations with very good grades I hoped to be able to work as a secretary. I still liked the idea of working at De Bijenkorf, but the owners were Jewish, and by the time I'd started my search for a job they'd already been sent away, along with the Jewish staff.

The only employment I could find was at a company just fifteen minutes from our house, but after my first day Pa found out that it involved putting filters on cigarettes and he put his foot down: his daughter was not going to do unskilled work! So I never went back.

He did succeed in finding me another position – working for a German refugee named Mittwoch who had his own fashion house. So I started my first job. I mainly helped out in the office and assisted the bookkeeper, but I was also required to model clothes when we took them to shops. Fortunately I had a good figure. We only went to Jewish businesses, but since many fashion houses and clothes shops were owned by Jews there was plenty of demand for Mittwoch's clothing.

It could have been a fun job because, like lots of young women, I was interested in fashion, but Mittwoch was a difficult man. He was a stickler for punctuality and didn't spare a thought for my circumstances – because Jews were no longer permitted to use public transport, it would take me almost an hour to walk from our house in De Pijp to his canal-side premises on the Keizersgracht. If I arrived a couple of minutes late he was furious, even though he expected me to work until after seven o'clock every evening, when my hours were officially eight thirty to five thirty.

Every evening around six he liked to eat an apple and would offer me one too, but otherwise he showed no interest whatsoever in my wellbeing. I soon became fed up and decided to look for another job.

Mittwoch received a weekly copy of *Het Joodsche Weekblad*, the Jewish newspaper, which was still printed at the time. All German regulations relating to Jews were published in it, so Jewish families bought it to stay up to date. One day I was leafing through it and saw an advert for a job as a secretary at a paper company not far from where we lived.

That evening, Mittwoch tried to bribe me again with an apple when it was already seven, so I threw the fruit at his head and said I was leaving. The next day I went to the paper company and was given the job. I can be very daring when I need to be, but thank God I had the courage to leave. It later transpired that changing jobs had saved my life.

The paper company belonged to a Jewish family called De Jong. The man was Dutch, his wife was a German refugee, and he had a ten-year-old daughter from a previous marriage. I liked the daughter very much and we soon became good friends. The company delivered all sorts of paper to offices and printers, and they operated the business from their home, using the spare room as an office. Officially, I was the secretary, but they asked me to help around the house too. Jewish families were no longer allowed to hire in help and Mrs De Jong had her hands full with the business. I agreed to the terms and we worked cheerfully side by side.

I had no way of knowing then that, like so many Dutch Jews, the De Jongs wouldn't survive the war. After the liberation I met Mrs De Jong's cousin, who told me they had been murdered. We were completely unprepared for what was to come. Despite the restrictions and the rumours about what might happen, we still didn't realize that the Nazis wanted to wipe out all the Jews. But as time went on they adopted more and more measures to isolate us from the rest of society.

The February Strike took place in February 1941. It was targeted at all these anti-Semitic measures and was mainly organized by the communists and social democrats. Illegal newspapers, such as *De Waarheid* and *De Vonk* – which I later helped to distribute – had called on the people to stand up against the persecution of the Jews. Tram workers, railway staff and port labourers responded first, followed by other workers. However, the Germans soon nipped the protest in the bud and arrested countless participants. Men were shot dead, and a great many men and women were locked up. Later on, when I was in Ravensbrück, I discovered that a couple of my friends had been involved. We liked to hear about the things people had done to stand up to the Germans, and I thought the strike was a good thing to have been a part of.

Although the strike was suppressed, it was a powerful expression of resistance against Nazi activities. Many acts of resistance like it resulted in violent reprisals. After one particular German was shot, two hundred Jewish men were rounded up in dawn raids in retaliation and sent to the Mauthausen concentration camp in Austria – one of the first, largest and harshest labour camps, intended for the worst political enemies of the German occupier. These men were set to work, as it was termed, but two weeks later their families received word that they had succumbed to the elements. After the war we found out that they'd been left out naked in the snow to die of exposure, or shot if they tried to run away.

There were many more atrocities. The owner of an ice-cream parlour in our neighbourhood, for example, refused to serve a German soldier. In response, the soldier returned with an officer who forced the parlour owner outside, put him up against the wall and shot him dead.

On 13 February 1941, the German authorities set up the Jewish Council, deploying its members to make contact with the Jewish community and convey their anti-Semitic measures. The chairmen of the Jewish Council, Abraham Asscher and David Cohen, thought that by cooperating they might be able to prevent the situation from deteriorating, but to no avail – the Jews only had more restrictions imposed on them.

In September 1943, Asscher and Cohen were arrested and

deported, although – unlike almost all the other Jews – they weren't sent to extermination camps: Asscher was sent to Bergen-Belsen and Cohen to Theresienstadt, where prisoners had a better chance of survival.

After the war, the pair were severely criticized and accused of having helped the Nazis. The Dutch government conducted an investigation into their presumed collaboration and in 1947 they were banned from ever holding office in the Dutch Jewish community again. They were both exonerated in 1950 in response to protests. It was accepted that they, like so many others, had sincerely believed that the Jews were being sent to work camps in Eastern Europe, rather than to the savage torture and murder camps where they really ended up.

In January 1941 all Jews – that is, anyone with four Jewish grandparents – were ordered to register with the Dutch authorities. The following month, the Germans put up barbed wire around the Jewish quarter, so that they could control the food supply. During the course of April, May and June that year we were prohibited from making use of public transport and facilities such as theatres, cinemas, hotels, restaurants and swimming pools. We were denied all sources of amusement and there was little we were permitted to do outside the home. The one thing I was allowed to go to was a weekly Jewish dance class.

Then came a new decree: we were to hand in our radios within fourteen days. It was a terrible blow. Cut off from the outside world as we already were, we were to lose our remaining point of contact, which was invaluable to us. Our upstairs neighbours' son lowered an aerial so that we could listen to public broadcasting and *Radio Oranje* via the BBC in London on a little radio, but we stopped when we felt it was becoming too dangerous to do so.

Between 8 and 11 August 1941 we had to register our property with the Lipmann-Rosenthal Bank. This bank, known as the Liro, was a renowned institution under Jewish ownership. The Germans, however, had seized it in order to confiscate Jewish possessions. Everything had to be handed in there: share certificates, insurance policies, property deeds. It was clever of the Nazis, as the Liro, which of course was no longer a real bank, continued to use the Lipmann-Rosenthal letterhead for all receipts and communications; most people thought the old bank was still in business and were confident they would eventually get their money back.

The following year, in May 1942, besides all our valuable papers we also had to hand in our physical property, and one of the bank's offices became a depot for our possessions. Works of art, jewellery and furniture had to be given up, as well as everyday items such as household utensils and bicycles – anything from which the Nazis could profit. No object was too small – even teaspoons were seized. This robbery was so well organized that a Liro bank was set up in the transit camp in Westerbork. Jews who arrived there had to hand in their possessions to be placed 'in storage' before they were sent to extermination camps in Poland.

The segregation of the Jews progressed systematically. In September 1941 Clara had to leave her school for a Jewish one. On 23 January 1942 the Jews had a big 'J' stamped on their identity cards to distinguish them from the rest of the population.

On 3 May all Jews aged six and over were ordered to wear a yellow Star of David with the word 'Jew' on it. The star had to be sewn on at chest height, so that we were easy to spot.

That was a horrible moment – we realized just how stigmatized we were. It felt as if we were being branded, and that I was being forced to attest that I was 'different' from my fellow Dutch citizens; as if we had a terrible disease and everyone else was safe only if they could see our mark and keep their distance.

Our whole family wore the star; after all, the order stated that if we didn't then we would be arrested and shot. I hated that thing and held my bag over it so it wasn't easily visible. Every act of resistance, however small, was important to me.

In June, a curfew was imposed and Jews were no longer allowed on the streets between eight o'clock in the evening and six in the morning. After that, things went from bad to worse. On 14 July 1942, seven hundred Jews were rounded up in Amsterdam, and the following day, transport of Jews to the concentration camps of Westerbork in the Netherlands and Auschwitz in occupied Poland began.

The Germans started arresting boys and girls in the street and sent them in cattle wagons – via Amsterdam Central Station and Westerbork – to Eastern Europe, where they were supposedly put to work. Now we know the horrific truth, but back then, in our innocence, we were unaware. The first groups even went to their deaths singing, with guitars and violins in their hands. Many of them were murdered immediately, but some were first compelled to work and then starved or beaten to death.

I still remember Uncle Levi asking my father, 'Barend, what do you think they do with the Jews in Poland?'

'They probably make mincemeat of them,' my father replied.

I was shocked. Previously his answer had always been, 'They'll be put to work. The Germans are too clever not to get as much use as possible out of them first. It would be foolish to slaughter them straight away.'

Despite these events, which left us feeling ever more desperate, life simply went on. For instance, I had a friend, Clara Cardozo, whom I saw almost every day. We chatted and spent our time as young women do. Our families were good friends, and Pa played cards with her father and brothers. The Cardozos belonged to my mother's side of the family and came from Roermond in the southeast of the Netherlands, but since Clara's father's fashion house had been seized and they'd had to move to Amsterdam, they now lived in a magnificent, spacious apartment on Zuider Amstellaan (now Rooseveltlaan). Besides our daily meetings, I also saw her each week at my Jewish dance class.

I saw my cousin Loutje at the class too, and I was very attached to him. He'd become such a charming young man: tall, slim and handsome. He'd been back living with his father, Uncle Jacques, and his stepmother, Aunt Tini, from the start of 1941, following his stay in the children's home in Leiden. He'd taken a vocational course in fashion and specialized in tailoring shirts, and when he moved back home he taught his father everything he knew about shirt-making. Together they started a successful business.

Loutje and I were very similar in age, and we spent lots of time together. At dance class we often danced together. I can no longer imagine how we kept going with ordinary activities while inconceivable events were unfolding around us, but we were youthful and full of energy, and we couldn't sit back and wait for the worst. We were young, innocent people who didn't really grasp the seriousness of the situation for European Jews.

Gradually, however, the reality began to dawn on us. Just over a year later, in April 1942, Loutje, like so many other young people, was summoned to work in Eastern Europe. He came round to our house, and I'll never forget the conversation between him and my father. He asked Pa if he knew where he could get a pair of sturdy boots or shoes to take with him. It was difficult for anyone to buy good shoes or boots in the shops, and nigh on impossible if you were Jewish. Everyone still thought people were really being summoned to work and Loutje wanted to be well prepared.

Later, I discovered that he was sent to an extermination camp, and in 1943 he was murdered.

4

Away from Home: *A family in hiding*

Loutje's summons came as a wake-up call – before long we too would be taken away to a work camp.

Pa had me and Clara vaccinated against deadly diseases such as pneumonic plague and diphtheria. For some reason or other neither he nor Mams was vaccinated. They seemed to take their own health less seriously than ours.

I turned twenty on 7 June 1942. But what should have been a celebration became a sombre day, as I received the dreaded summons, demanding that I present myself at Amsterdam Central Station to be taken to a work camp in Eastern Europe. We didn't know at the time what happened to people in the camps, but of course the last thing I wanted was to leave my family behind and go away alone. I was really still a child.

To buy time, Pa gave me some laxative chocolate so that I got terrible diarrhoea. He called the doctor, who wrote a note stating that there was blood in my stool. I received a sickness *Sperre* – a document waiving my summons to join the transport to the work camp – but it was valid only for a couple of days; I needed a more permanent excuse.

You could obtain an exemption if you worked in certain

professions, such as nursing, so I decided to pretend I was a nurse. Dientje Jesse, a very good non-Jewish friend of my cousin Zetty Roet, had been a nurse before she got married, so I borrowed a uniform from her, put it on and went to the Department of Exemptions in Amsterdam-Zuid. In front of the building was a bench that served as a desk. There was a woman sitting behind it, with an SS officer standing at her side.

The queue was extremely long. I had to wait for hours on end, growing more and more nervous. I was afraid of the questions they would ask to find out whether I was telling the truth, but when it came to my turn the woman simply said it was against the rules to switch from a sickness *Sperre* to a social exemption. I was required to present myself for transport to Eastern Europe the following day.

I'd had high hopes for my plan, so I was desperately disappointed and made my way to Mr and Mrs De Jong immediately to tell them I could no longer work for them. When I arrived they were in the garden talking to their neighbour, a Jewish German emigrant who ran a fur factory and was mandated to make clothing for the German soldiers on the Russian front. He listened to my story and, to my amazement, said, 'Why don't you come and work for me?'

Since the kind of work I would be doing was deemed essential for the war, it meant I wouldn't have to go to Poland. I could hardly believe this sudden reversal of fortune. What a stroke of luck that never would have come had I not risked leaving Mittwoch and applying to the De Jongs! It wasn't the last time during the war that pure luck would save my life.

I went home relieved, and that evening our family did feel

we had something to celebrate on my birthday. Filled with joy, I presented myself for work at the fur factory the following morning and began to learn the trade, making mittens and other fur items.

Meanwhile, the danger continued to grow. One day Pa came home and told us that the Germans were arresting boys and young men in the street. He sent me to warn my cousins Maurits and David, Uncle Arie and Aunt Sara's sons. They lived fifteen minutes' walk from us. Looking back, I realize how strange that was. Girls were being arrested in the street just as boys were, but somehow no one in my family gave a thought to the risk I was taking in making the journey.

Although I was twenty, my family still saw me as a child. Since Clara and I were so much younger than Louis, David and our cousins, we were always seen as little girls, and when our parents and brothers went to family events, the two of us stayed home and waited for them to return from the party with cakes. So it didn't occur to my father – nor me, in fact – that I might be in danger when I went out. Only on my way home, when I saw boys and girls being loaded into trucks, did I realize how risky it was. I covered my Star of David and fled homewards, my heart in my mouth, praying the Germans wouldn't catch sight of me.

Uncle Arie and Aunt Sara had been trying for some time to travel to Switzerland with their son Maurits, who was already married. After my warning they made another attempt. Maurits' father-in-law was a wealthy diamond merchant, so their family had a large sum of money to pay anyone who could help them cross the border. They waited in a café for their smuggler as instructed, but instead of being brought to safety they were arrested by the German police. The man to whom they'd paid so much money had betrayed them.

I assume that informers didn't know then of the deadly consequences of their betrayal – they were just greedy. In addition to the money from the Jews they'd offered to help, they would have also received a reward of seven guilders for each Jew they turned in. That was a lot of money in those days – as much as a week's welfare payments – and the temptation for some was simply too great.

For Jewish people it was impossible to know who you could trust, but Uncle Arie and his family were so desperate that they'd taken the risk. After their arrest the German police sent them home, but a couple of weeks later they were captured during the systematic round-up of Jews. Their eldest son, David, who was studying medicine, had gone into hiding in a fellow student's house in Hilversum. He should have been safe. But one evening he decided to go home to fetch some books. That very evening the family was arrested by the *Sicherheitsdienst* – the Nazi intelligence and security service – and transported to Auschwitz. David too. We never saw any of them again.

Whether people lived or died often depended on a coincidental split-second decision. My father had also talked about fleeing to Switzerland, but after what happened to Uncle Arie and his family, he no longer had the courage. And at that point we didn't know what happened to the people who were transported to Eastern Europe. We still thought they were going to work camps.

Meanwhile, the Allies were dropping bombs. One landed

close to our house – fortunately, it destroyed only the window. Despite the danger, we welcomed the bombs. After all, we knew that the Allied forces were fighting to destroy the Nazis and we lived in the naive hope that the war would soon be over. But it only came closer.

Four months after I'd been called up, my father was the next to be summoned to present himself for a work camp in Drenthe. Perhaps we could have come up with another ruse, but rumour had it that if the man of the family went, his wife and children would be exempt. We believed it – just as we believed all the lies we were told – so Pa decided it was better to go.

Our hearts broke at parting, but on 2 October he set off for the assembly point in good spirits. We were anxious, naturally, but we genuinely thought he would be put to work – maybe on a farm, or in a factory. We were afraid for him, but there was nothing we could do to change the situation, and we had every reason to believe we would see him again. It was crushing for us to hear that a day after his arrival in Drenthe he was sent straight on to the Westerbork transit camp. We hadn't seen that coming. Was he not deemed strong enough to work? After the war I heard that all the men were sent from the work camp to the transit camp.

Westerbork was built in 1939 by the Dutch government to receive Jewish refugees from Germany – it was intended for humanitarian purposes. Ironically, this made things easier for the Nazis. By the time the Germans invaded the Netherlands, more than seven hundred Jews were already living in the camp. The isolated location also worked to their advantage:

the roads were untarmacked, and when it rained the sand soon turned to mud, making the camp even less accessible.

Westerbork was initially overseen by the Dutch government, but as soon as it came under German authority it was easy for the Nazis to turn it into a transit camp for Jews. They surrounded the site with a barbed-wire fence and seven watchtowers, and erected wooden barracks. In the end, there were 107 barracks, each of which could accommodate three hundred people. Those about to be transported were permitted to bring one suitcase or rucksack each, labelled with their name, date of birth and 'Netherlands'. My father had already bought us large rucksacks, following advice to Jews in case they were suddenly sent to Eastern Europe.

At first sight, daily life in Westerbork seemed reasonably tolerable. The camp was partly run by selected Jewish leaders, and offered access to healthcare, education and sport, with a cabaret once a week. The illusion of ordinary life was so well maintained that my cousin Sarah – whom I had visited with Grandma at the Jewish orphanage – even got married there. She had come to Amsterdam in 1941 to work as a housekeeper for a young rabbi in Haarlem, and had fallen in love with him. When he was transported to Westerbork early in the summer of 1942, Sarah, who was half Jewish and therefore didn't have to join the transport, chose to go with him.

We know that Pa spent some time at the hospital in Westerbork, although I'm not sure why. At first I thought he might be pretending to be unwell because it was more comfortable and safer in the hospital barracks, but later I heard that he had actually been gravely ill. I wonder whether he was perhaps suffering from alcohol withdrawal. In any case, he was permitted to send us a card once a month.

We also received news through friends and family who worked at Westerbork and were allowed to leave the camp regularly – if they worked for the Jewish Council they could come home every weekend. I even sent Pa chocolate, which, as we'll see later, saved my life. This illusion of normality was upheld so that people would remain calm and not rebel, and I think it worked. The prisoners thought that if they cooperated they would have a good chance of remaining safe, but it was all a façade.

Between July 1942 and September 1944 trains left Westerbork every Tuesday to transport Jews to extermination camps. No one was exempt. My cousin Sarah and her husband were taken along with everyone else and murdered. If she hadn't chosen to go with him, she might have survived the war, being half Jewish, but who can blame her for wanting to stay with the man she loved? Sixty-five trains full of Jews set off from Westerbork for Auschwitz, where most of the prisoners were gassed soon after disembarking; nineteen trains left for Sobibor, where everyone was gassed on arrival; and then there were the trains to Bergen-Belsen and Theresienstadt. Almost a hundred and seven thousand Dutch Jews travelled these routes to their deaths.

The same evening Pa was taken to Drenthe, I was woken by the sound of heavy German boots pounding up the stairs. I stayed in bed with Clara, and we hugged each other for comfort. My heart was thumping. I thought they were coming for us, but they took a family from one of the other apartments. Clearly we weren't on their list that night.

The strange thing is, although I was scared, I took out my curlers in case we were to be transported. The vanity of a young woman! It seems inconceivable that anyone would think of such a thing at a moment like that, but it's the honest truth. We didn't know what was happening to our neighbours, but we heard people screaming.

'They're coming for us tomorrow,' I said to my mother, terrified.

The sound of people being taken away is frightening. The German SS officers and the Dutch police made a racket as they marched up the stairs, banging on doors and ordering everyone, young and old, to come out as quickly as possible. The Germans yelled at people, kicked and beat them, without any consideration for illness, age or frailty. They threw them into trucks with the help of the Dutch police.

A great many were taken away to the Hollandsche Schouwburg, a theatre in the heart of the old Jewish quarter, and sent to Westerbork from there. The venue had been built in 1892, and had enjoyed great success in the 1930s with serious plays, revues and operettas. Many German and Austrian Jewish artists had fled to the Netherlands and performed there, alongside Eastern European Jewish refugees.

It was a lively theatre, and the performances it put on were high quality, but not long after the German occupation the anti-Semitic measures began to make their mark. The place was renamed the Joodsche Schouwburg (the Jewish theatre) and Jews were forbidden from performing for a non-Jewish audience. Ironically, the theatre was so popular that non-Jews borrowed Stars of David to get in.

LEFT: *The passport photo of Barend Velleman, Pa. Circa 1931.*

RIGHT: *The passport photo of Femmetje Spier, Mams. Circa 1942.*

Mams, Pa, Selma (aged four or five), David (thirteen) and Louis (fifteen, standing). Circa 1926.

ABOVE LEFT: *Newspaper article with the caption, 'Now that's really something: milk with a straw. You only have to look at the pupils' faces to see how much they are enjoying it …' Clara in the foreground, 24 January 1939.*

ABOVE RIGHT: *Selma and Clara. Diemen,* circa *1930.*

BELOW: *Femmetje (Mams), Clara, Jo Grobfeld, who was a great friend, and Selma (left to right). Diemen, 1930.*

ABOVE: *Selma with Jo Grobfeld and Frieda Twelkemeyer, a school friend (left to right). Amsterdam, 3 June 1937.*

LEFT: *Clara (eleven), Jan Lievensstraat, Amsterdam, 1939. Photo taken by Selma with her Lumière camera.*

Selma (left) on her birthday, with cousins Janni (centre) and Emily (who died in 1943). Jan Lievensstraat, Amsterdam, June 1940.

Left: *Brother David in uniform, London.* Circa *1940.*

Right: *Brother Louis in uniform, London, 11 October 1941.*

Mams, Pa, Clara, Selma (right). Amsterdam, October 1941.

Selma in hiding at the Oude Singel in Leiden, May 1943.

The next chapter of the Hollandsche Schouwburg's history devastating. In 1942 and 1943, thousands of Jewish men, women and children were rounded up there to be transported to Westerbork. Few returned. My cousin David Roet – who was in the sanatorium in Laren in 't Gooi at the same time as I was – probably met his death that way, and doubtless other family members did too.

The theatre is now a memorial, with the names of all the murdered Dutch Jews listed on the walls. Inside, you can hear recordings of accounts by a number of performers from the time. An actress tells the chilling story of the evening before the theatre was closed: .

> There was a Nazi backstage inspecting everything without touching anything. He tiptoed around in silence. He said to me, 'Don't mind me, I hope I'm not disturbing you.' Everyone wondered what he was doing there. We talked about it and decided he thought perhaps something was up. The next day he returned and told us the theatre was closed and was now a deportation centre. He said if we objected we could volunteer to leave with the first transport.

The theatre really had two functions: it was used as a deportation centre, but also as a place to keep Jews imprisoned for longer periods. The building was completely unsuitable for this purpose, and the people held there spoke of how overcrowded it was, the sickening stench, and how desperately fearful those locked up there felt.

Walter Süskind, who had fled from Germany to the Netherlands in 1938, was the theatre manager at the time. I met him when he was part of the Westerweel Group (a resistance group), but at that point I had no idea what he did. Süskind used his position to save Jewish children from a crèche opposite the theatre. He conspired with the people who worked there to rescue as many infants as possible by smuggling them in bags or rucksacks to other parts of the Netherlands, where they were taken in by non-Jewish families. Süskind made sure their names were removed from the paperwork – so that the Nazis wouldn't know they'd ever existed – and around six hundred children were saved this way. Süskind's wife, Johanna, and his daughter, Yvonne, were murdered in Auschwitz in October 1944. Walter himself died on 28 February 1945 during one of the death marches.

The day after Mams, Clara and I escaped notice by the Germans by the skin of our teeth, I realized that something had to happen if we didn't want to end up in the Hollandsche Schouwburg. My mother was incapable of making plans. She had no idea what to do. Pa had always made the important decisions for the family, and before him her parents and older siblings had done the same.

My parents might still have seen me as a child, but I had my father's character. I was strong-willed and decisive. When I was confronted with this terrible challenge I knew I had to behave like an adult and do what was best for my mother and Clara. I decided we should go into hiding. It was October 1942.

The resistance movement was still in its infancy and it was difficult to find addresses where we could hide, but I had an idea. My friend Clara Cardozo had told me in secret that she wouldn't be at our dance class the following week because she was going away with her family. I knew she meant they were going into hiding or leaving the country.

She lived with her father, brothers and sister-in-law in a large apartment on Amstellaan, but her sister-in-law wasn't going with them, Clara told me. I never asked why not and can only guess. Her brother's wife didn't look Jewish because she was blonde, as was her three-year-old daughter. Perhaps she was told she had a better chance of survival living openly as a non-Jew than in hiding with her in-laws, who were all dark-haired and looked very Jewish.

When my mother agreed to the plan to go into hiding, I went to Clara's sister-in-law in the hope that she might have contacts who could help. She gave me the details of a man who'd sold them addresses, and he turned out to be someone I already knew: our insurance agent.

It was very expensive to go into hiding – there were few people who were prepared to take in refugees without being paid. So I called the people in Middelburg with whom my brother David was initially billeted – the Jongeneels. My father had left some money and jewellery with them early on, when Jews were banned from keeping such items. Mrs Jongeneel, who had since become a good friend, came to us with the sum I'd requested.

The next day our insurance agent told us that my mother and Clara should go to the train station and travel south. They were to stay in Eindhoven with a woman who had three children – a boy and two girls. I later discovered that her husband lived with his mistress, which is why she was alone with the children. I didn't go with Mams and Clara – there was only space for two and it would have cost too much.

So Mams and Clara left Amsterdam, and I remained in the city to survive alone. It was an impossible situation. I had no idea when I would see them again, but there were too many things to sort out to be consumed with grief. I had to focus on myself. To raise some money I'd sold all our kitchenware to my mother's friend Jo Nijland. She gave me two guilders for it, and although it was a paltry sum, I was full of joy at having some cash. That shows how desperate I was. I also had to find somewhere to live.

When I was still at school, I'd gone to evening classes to learn shorthand and typing, and had made friends with a fellow student. She also lived with her family in a large apartment on Amstellaan. When things had started looking really bad for the Jews, she'd said to me, 'If you ever need a place to stay, come to us.' So I did indeed go to her, lugging a big suitcase of clothes behind me.

There were five children and the apartment was jam-packed – we shared a bedroom. I remember being shocked that my hosts all slept in their underwear. However poor my family had been, we'd always slept in pyjamas. The family was fairly well off – they had to be to live at that address – yet none of the children had any nightclothes. In hindsight, I realize I was quite prejudiced, but it also shows that my parents had always taken care to maintain a certain standard of living, however difficult it must have been to do so.

A couple of days after I'd moved in, the mother mentioned that they were running out of coal and food. My father had built up a big supply to last the war, so I told her what we had and we went to fetch it. Just a week later she explained that it

was becoming dangerous to have me in the house and that I'd
have to leave that evening.

'But you have all our coal and food,' I said in my innocence.

'Oh, that's all gone,' she replied.

She was lying, of course, but given that I could hardly lug
the coal and food around with me, there was nothing for it but
to accept the situation. I left that evening, dragging my suitcase behind me once more. I felt betrayed. It had been naive of
my friend to offer help, and of course it wasn't safe for them to
keep me there – 'We have five children to think of,' the mother
had said – but I was deeply disappointed.

I wandered the streets with my possessions like a nomad.
The only thing I could think of was to go to Uncle Jacques and
Aunt Tini, who lived about fifteen minutes' walk away. They
took me in. Loutje had already been summoned to the work
camp in Eastern Europe by that point, so I slept in his old
room. If I'd known then what had happened to him, it would
have been unbearable.

I was still in touch with Pa during this difficult period. My
cousin Zetty's sister-in-law worked at the Westerbork Jewish
Council office, and Pa wrote to tell me that I could go to her
to find out how he was doing. When we met in Amsterdam
she gave me the object that was to become my most cherished possession: Pa's black Waterman fountain pen. I
recognized it immediately, as it was the one he'd always used.
Seeing it took me back to old times: Pa writing letters and
notes; the whole family at home. I was delighted that he'd
asked Zetty's sister-in-law to give it to me. I saw it as a

talisman – it felt like having Pa with me, and I was determined not to lose it.

Although Pa himself was in such a precarious situation, he was still thinking of others. He asked me to take some money to two very poor elderly ladies every week. When I did, they told me he'd been doing so for years, despite the fact that we often had little money ourselves.

The one thing he asked me to do for him was to send him some chocolates. I thought it an odd request, as he didn't have a sweet tooth, but it was at that point that Zetty's sister-in-law explained that he'd been seriously ill and was in the infirmary. Apparently, he wanted the chocolates for the nurses. I suspect he was bribing them to let him stay longer – it was probably safer there than being in the camp and running the risk of being transported to Eastern Europe.

I made sure to buy huge boxes of chocolates from the man Pa had recommended, and sent them regularly. Surprisingly, they were accepted by the camp and did reach Pa. This was just one of the many unimaginable examples of the way the Germans did things. A prisoner could be permitted to receive gifts one day, then transported to another camp and murdered the next.

I was still working at the fur factory, and one morning I set out early to get to the post office before work. I'd just sent a package of chocolates and cheese to Pa and was on my way to the factory when I felt uneasy. I can't explain it – I simply had a gut instinct that something wasn't right. A nervous feeling in my tummy. I reached the corner of the street, but then, anxious, I decided to return to Uncle Jacques' house instead.

A couple of hours later I heard that that very day – 11 November 1942 – the *Sicherheitsdienst*, led by its chief Willy Lages, had raided the factory. The exits were blocked and the employees were arrested and deported to concentration camps. If I hadn't followed my instincts, I would have been among them. I couldn't believe it – an enormous feeling of guilt and relief washed over me when the rumours were confirmed, and I started to tremble. I had escaped – again. But the feeling of anxiety didn't leave me.

Years later, after the war, I ran into one of the two brothers who owned the factory. He told me he'd fled to the toilets when he heard the trucks arrive. The others, including his brother, were all taken outside and forced into the trucks. None of them were ever seen again. If my father had known my life had been saved because I was out doing something for him, he'd have been very moved. In the end, he never came to know his family's fate.

On 6 December 1942, while I was staying with Uncle Jacques and Aunt Tini, I received a message that Pa had been sent to Auschwitz. He was murdered there on 7 December, although I only found that out several months after the end of the war. For a long time the authorities didn't know what had happened to him. I was already living in England when I was told. Of course, all that time I'd hoped he was still alive. I knew Pa had a strong survival instinct, and I'd heard so many stories of people who'd escaped that I held out hope until the unthinkable message arrived.

At the time, I lived in terrible fear because I didn't know where my family were or how they were doing. Once the fur factory had been closed down I no longer had a job, so I went to look after my cousin David Roet's children. David's girl-friend, Riekie, had become pregnant in 1939, but his parents were against their marriage. He didn't have a job and they dis-approved of Riekie's background – they didn't think she was good enough for him. She wasn't educated, and was often ill with tuberculosis.

I knew the family well, and David used to spend quite a bit of time at our house. He was good friends with my brothers and had always felt more at home with us than with his own family. In May 1940, when he told my father about Riekie's pregnancy, Pa organized a get-together at our house for David, Riekie, and David's parents, Levi and Jaan. The nights leading up to the meeting, Riekie slept in my bed, and I slept in the spare room.

My father, as always an honourable man, had told my uncle and aunt that it was David's duty to marry Riekie, especially given that it was what the young couple wanted. So they were married, a second child was born, and in 1942 Riekie was pregnant with their third. She was taken to the Jewish hospital early on in her pregnancy because of her tuberculosis, and it was while she was there that I began going to their house each day to look after their other two children. It was another new job for me, and would lead to my first contribution to the resistance.

Dientje Jesse, the woman who'd lent me the nurse's uni-form, lived around the corner from Uncle Jacques. Despite growing up in Catholic Limburg, she'd had a strict Protestant upbringing, but she herself wasn't religious and had been desperate to leave home. She found a job in a shoe shop in Alkmaar and it was there that she met Bob Jesse.

She and Bob were married shortly before the war broke out and moved to a lovely apartment in Amsterdam. Dientje had decorated it in a modern style, with orange lino in the bedroom. She was so proud of it that you had to take off your shoes before you set foot inside. At the time, most women had to give up their jobs when they got married, and Dientje was no exception, so she put all her time into the apartment and, as I was to discover later, into the resistance.

I met Dientje and Bob through my cousins David and Zetty Roet. Both couples were around ten years older than me. I didn't know them particularly well, but they helped me when I was in need during the war and we became very good friends. Bob was half Jewish and he and Dientje had many Jewish friends who needed fake documents and addresses to go into hiding. That was why they started to work for the resistance, which was just getting off the ground at the time. They used supposedly lost identity cards for their purposes, which they obtained in all manner of ways. In the early days, Bob removed the photos from the 'lost' cards using a very primitive technique and then stuck new ones on.

One day, Dientje asked me to visit Riekie in hospital, where she was on the maternity ward with her new baby, Levi. I was to keep her talking for as long as possible after she'd fed him, so that Dientje, dressed in her nurse's uniform, could take him away. Instead of returning him to the nursery, Dientje would take him into hiding. Babies were separated temporarily from their mothers back then – in an infant ward – so she wouldn't have thought anything untoward was happening. Riekie wasn't allowed to know anything about our plan, as she would certainly have screamed and protested and refused to give him up.

Many Jewish parents didn't want their children taken away. They didn't realize what would happen to them, and had no sense of the danger they faced. It had to be done on the sly, to keep the hospital employees – who were secretly in on it – from danger as well. Once Levi was successfully removed, Dientje told Riekie what we'd done and why. She had no choice but to accept it and remain in hospital on her own. I didn't see her again, but can only assume that while she would have been distraught that her baby was gone, she would eventually have felt relief that he had been saved.

Levi was renamed George, placed with a Catholic miner's family in Limburg, and was very well cared for. After the war he went to Israel. Riekie and David's other two children, whom I had been looking after, were also placed with Christian foster parents. All three survived the war; sadly their mother and father did not. Soon after Levi's removal, the Jewish hospital was emptied and Riekie was taken on a transport to Auschwitz.

This was my first tentative contribution to the resistance and the first time I realized that it existed. I still didn't know much about the movement, but this incident provided a hint of what went on and I became involved without being fully aware. At that point I had no idea of the extent to which I would come to participate in resistance activities; I was still thinking primarily of my own safety. It was only later that I began to think seriously about how I could help others.

Meanwhile, I was struggling to survive financially. The money Pa had left with Mrs Jongeneel in Middelburg was beginning to run out. I was still receiving money deducted from Louis's wages, which a bookkeeper from the Hollandsche Stoomboot Maatschappij delivered each month to my mother's friend Jo Nijland. I met this bookkeeper at Jo's place to receive the money, but after a while 'Aunt' Jo said it was getting too dangerous: her neighbour had a friend in the National Socialist Movement who couldn't be trusted. So because there was no other safe place where I could meet the bookkeeper, that source of income came to a halt. After liberation, I went to see the bookkeeper, but he shut the door in my face. He'd probably pocketed the money himself. When Louis found out that the money deducted from his wages throughout the war had never reached me, he was furious.

I had to find a way of earning money so that I could pay Uncle Jacques and Aunt Tini for board and lodging. I couldn't expect them to feed me and offer me a room for nothing. Although Jacques was trying to make shirts for his private customers, it was such a slow process without Loutje that it was difficult for him to make ends meet. Aunt Tini, who wasn't Jewish, dealt with sales and delivery of the shirts, which Jews were prohibited from doing. But even though the shirts were made from expensive fabric, which Jacques had bought at a high price on the black market, he couldn't sell them for much.

David Roet and his friend Hartog Hammelburg came to

my aid. They hired a cart, loaded some of my family's furniture and paintings onto it and sold them for a couple of guilders. I was relieved to have some money, however little, so I could pay for my food. And at least this way our possessions didn't go to the Nazis. Although there were still many items of furniture and clothing, and other things in our apartment, I never saw them again. I often wonder what happened to them.

Though I had come up with a bit of extra cash, I wasn't able to stay with my aunt and uncle for long. Aunt Tini, who had always been a nervous woman, was becoming increasingly anxious at my presence. Her voice became higher and higher, until she seemed quite hysterical. A curfew had been imposed on everyone, unless you had a special pass that gave you permission to be out and about after eight in the evening, and the blackout curtains had to be closed so that no light could be seen from outside. The employees of the air raid protection force, many of whom sympathized with the Nazi regime, could come along at any time to inspect the premises.

One evening, the doorbell rang a little after eight. Jacques and Tini's apartment was on the top floor, so I climbed out of the window in my room and onto the roof. I lay down flat in the gutter in the pouring rain to hide myself from view. Sometimes the air raid protection officer would not only come to the house, but would go into my room and switch on the light. On this occasion, it turned out that the officer had come round simply to inform people of new regulations, and my uncle said he was a kind enough chap. However, his supposedly well-meaning visits persisted, and my aunt grew more and more nervous.

Another time he came and I climbed onto the roof as usual.

I lay there for an eternity, in the evening rain, shivering with cold and terror. I saw the air raid inspector turn the lights on and off in every room and peer through the windows. I was afraid he might spot me, so I jumped across to the next roof and hid there instead. I just lay there, waiting for him to go, trying to be completely silent and still. I have always had an enormous amount of self-control. When something is necessary, I do it.

These incidents, which kept happening with greater frequency, now seem so unimaginable that I often think I must have dreamt them. They seem more like something out of a film than real life, and it feels like an amazing feat to have evaded capture time and time again. But I was a young girl. I was fit and strong. It was an enormous risk to be up on the rooftop, but it had to be done. It wasn't just dangerous for me, though, but also for Jacques and Tini. As a Jew married to a Christian, my uncle was currently free, but if it were discovered that he was hiding me, he would have been deported, and Tini would have suffered the same fate. We didn't know about the concentration camps yet, but we still didn't want to be caught. There was a very real sense of danger.

A couple of days after the most recent unexpected visit, Uncles Jacques said he thought it would be better if I were to leave. He was terribly worried about Tini's nerves and feared she might accidentally let something slip. It was easy to say the wrong thing and many people were unintentionally betrayed in this way.

Uncle Jacques stayed with me in London after the war, and I learned that he'd been protected up to a point by his marriage to Tini. However, Jewish men married to non-Jewish women were summoned for sterilization, and twice he had been taken to the hospital for the procedure. Both times the doctors postponed the operation and found medical reasons to send him home without carrying it out. Evidently they were humane doctors who did everything in their power to protect him.

Filled with despair at losing my place to live, I went back to the insurance agent who had found a hiding place for Mams and Clara, and asked him to look for an address for me. He found a place in a working-class neighbourhood in the Jordaan – in the centre of the city – with a young couple who had newborn twins. I packed my big suitcase again and set off for their tiny third-floor apartment. Of course, a young woman walking around with a big suitcase must have looked very suspicious. I worried that people were probably looking at me and wondering what I was doing, but there wasn't much I could do about it. It was dangerous – I knew that. I covered my Star of David as best I could and somehow I got away with it.

In order to keep all of us as safe as possible, I had to pretend to be someone else. From that point on, it was time to leave behind my real self and begin to assume different roles. During my time with the couple in the Jordaan, I was supposedly the husband's sister from the north. The man of the house was very tall and blond, and had been put to work on the construction of the Boschplan, which later became the Amsterdamse Bos park.

In order to survive it was essential I couldn't be recognized as a Jew. Although I wasn't tall, I was now very blonde indeed – Uncle Jacques's brother owned a luxury hair salon and I'd had my hair bleached there. Like Uncle Jacques, he was married to a non-Jewish woman, which meant he was able to continue to run his business. He bleached my hair outside opening hours, when there were no other customers around.

My pretend brother and his wife were lovely people – it was a pleasure to stay with them. There were only two rooms in the apartment, though: I slept in the living room, and they slept and ate in the back room with the babies. This was typical of the sacrifices many non-Jews made to save Jewish lives, and I tried to go out as much as possible to give them their privacy.

My bed there was a divan brought down from the attic. It was reasonably comfortable, but after a couple of nights I was covered in red lumps and thought I'd caught some disease. I went to Dientje for a diagnosis and she told me they were flea bites. I'd never seen fleas before. She gave me something to protect me, but there were thousands of them in that divan, so nothing helped.

After a couple of months I bumped into Hartog Hammelburg – David Roet's friend, who had helped me to sell some of my family's furniture and paintings – in the street. He warned me not to go back to the Jordaan. The insurance agent who had found me a hiding place had tried to negotiate with the *Sicherheitsdienst*, he explained – the man had offered to give the SD the names of all the Jews he'd helped in exchange for the freedom of his wife and children.

I suspect the *Sicherheitsdienst* had come round to arrest him and his family and then found the lists, but as with so many other things, we'll never know the truth. What's certain is that he and his family were deported to Auschwitz, so even if he did negotiate in his desperation, it was for nothing. A number of Jews from his list were found and arrested, among them the whole Cardozo family, including my friend Clara.

It was clear that I might be next, so Hartog said I could stay with him. He borrowed a bed and put it in his room in lodgings on a side street off Ferdinand Bolstraat. Hartog had been a reputable pastry chef in Alkmaar – where he'd met Zetty and David, and Dientje and Bob – and was a very good cook. He succeeded in obtaining flour, butter and eggs on the black market, and baked in the passageway where there was an oven and a sink. It was wonderful for me because I'd not learned even the basics of cooking, thanks to the emphasis Pa put on my academic development.

Hartog and I shared some delicious meals, and we also often played chess. Staying with him was great fun. The only thing was, I'd failed to notice that he'd fallen in love with me. I was extremely innocent for my age and had no idea. Our beds were positioned across from each other, and one night he climbed in with me. I pretended to be asleep and allowed him to touch me all over because I had no idea how to deal with it. When he went too far I simply pushed him away, still pretending I was asleep.

A couple of nights later it happened again. This time, when he overstepped the mark, I acted as if I'd suddenly woken up and told him to leave me be. The next day, I went to Dientje to tell her what had happened and she found somewhere else for me to live. It was the end of 1942 and although I didn't know it yet, that was the start of my active participation in the resistance.

This story has a sting in the tail, which still haunts me. Hartog was a very sensitive man and, after the war, Dientje told me that he was so distressed I had left without a word that he went out into the street and wandered around until he was arrested. He died in Auschwitz.

Before he got himself arrested, he took all his money and possessions to Dientje and told her to give them to me. When the war was over, Hartog's sister visited Dientje. She'd just had a baby with an American soldier who had returned to the United States, and now she was alone with the infant. Dientje gave her all of Hartog's possessions.

When I learned about his fate, I felt very bad about it. To wander the streets like that had been a stupid thing for him to do, but I felt awful that I was the cause of his distress. I still feel awful about it, even after all this time.

5

Bleached Hair: *In the resistance*

So that was how I lived, as a non-Jewish blonde woman without a place to call home. At that point, my life took a fresh turn because I met two people. Dr Wim Storm was the head of the neurology department at the university hospital in Leiden, and he was deeply involved in the resistance. He found places for Jews to hide out, delivered the illegal Jewish babies of women in hiding, and helped people escape to Friesland, where he knew lots of sympathetically disposed farmers.

There were also non-Jews who needed help, because they were involved in illegal protest groups, for instance, or had refused to sign the declaration of loyalty to the Nazi regime. They all had to go into hiding and Wim helped them too, supplying them with food and identity documents. He was a short, rather plump man, with smooth, pink skin, and all the girls in the resistance were head over heels in love with him. He could get them to do anything, inspiring them to take big risks in carrying out their resistance activities. I admired him enormously for all his noble work, but I was never in love with him.

Ann de Lange, his wife – or the woman he lived with, at any rate – had worked for the resistance ever since measures against the Jews were introduced. She knew lots of influential people and had all sorts of useful contacts: designers and printers, as well as writers and journalists. From 1941 she had been involved in the publication of the illegal newspaper *De Vonk*, which I helped distribute between 1942 and 1944.

Both Wim and Ann became very good friends of mine. In December 1942 I received a gift from Ann: beautiful, salmon-pink silk pyjamas of hers that I'd admired. Such things were no longer available in the shops, and even if they had been, I'd never have been able to afford such a splurge.

Initially, I saw Wim simply as someone who helped me, because he'd been the one to take me to the new place Dientje had organized. It was the two upper floors of a canal-side house on the Oude Singel in Leiden, rented by two young women, Antje Holthuis and Mien Lubbe, who were colleagues of Wim's. Antje was a doctor and Mien was a medical lab technician.

Later, when Wim himself went into hiding because the Germans had found out about his activities, Antje took over from him as head of the neurology department, despite the fact that she was only twenty-three at the time. Like the other doctors in the hospital, she was involved in the resistance, and she and Mien were always ready to take Jewish people into hiding. Most stayed just a few days, but some, like me, remained for longer periods.

In May 1943, Lies (Alice) Kropveld, a twenty-seven-year-old teacher, also came to live in the Leiden canal house and stayed until after the liberation. She looked very Jewish and couldn't go out during the day, but when it was sunny she sat on the balcony at the back of the house where no one could see her. She was in love with a colleague who taught English with her at the secondary school in Leiden, and Wim helped them exchange letters.

Besides Dientje and Bob Jesse, Antje and Mien, Wim and Ann – and, of course, Greet – no one knew that I was Jewish. There were enough non-Jews in hiding that it didn't seem odd that I was there too. To further conceal my identity, I took the name of a student who had also lived in my room, Wilhelmina Buter. She was an American who had managed to return to the States just in time – I believe she left on the last ferry as the Germans invaded the Netherlands. She had a Dutch name, so must have had Dutch parents or grandparents who had emigrated. People said I looked a bit like her, and I was given an identity card with her name on it. I don't know if the resistance had produced that card, as other items of hers had also been left behind. My photo was stuck onto it, so this was the first time I lived fully as someone else.

It was essential that as few people as possible knew that I was Jewish; my safety depended on it. Only much later did it become clear to me how successful I'd been in keeping this secret, when Thea Boissevain, a friend with whom I was imprisoned at Ravensbrück, told me that a fellow prisoner had said she'd never trusted me because I never said anything about myself.

At the time, I knew nothing of the resistance work Antje and Mien did. I knew only that they were good people who had offered me refuge. In return, I helped them keep house, cooked a little, did the shopping and collected new food stamps. Every time I left the house I risked my life because I was Jewish, but I had to do it – so that we could all stay alive.

I did the shopping by bicycle, and every month I went to the municipal council for new food stamps. I also went to the soup kitchen, where you could obtain ready-made stew, almost every day. There was little gas or electricity, so these ready meals were a better option than home-cooking.

These seemingly everyday activities were as risky as the courier work I would take on later. One day, when I went to the municipal council, I had the fright of my life. I heard a man call out, 'Selma!' He was clearly someone who knew my real identity. I looked around and saw that it was Harry Groen, a man I had met at my cousins' house in Amsterdam. He was half Jewish and had grown up in the Jewish orphanage in Leiden, but my cousins had told me he was a traitor. It appeared that the Germans had given him a cart full of new brushes and cloths so that he could go from house to house selling them, and turn in all the Jews he came across.

When I saw him I thought my heart would give out. I grabbed my bike and rode home as fast as I could, glancing over my shoulder the whole way. Back home, I hid behind the curtain and peeked through the window. I saw him come over the nearby bridge with his handcart. Our house was to the right of the bridge and, to my immense relief, he turned left. I was terrified. Antje and Mien weren't home, so I didn't mention it to them, but I stayed indoors for the next couple of days, and for a while I was especially careful. Fortunately I never saw him again.

There was a third person in hiding with Lies and me: an

eighty-three-year-old Jewish man who hid in the annex. His name was Mr Weill, but we called him Grandpa. One day our paths crossed at the toilet. We chatted a little and he asked if I could play chess. After that, we met up to play the game a couple of times a week. He also taught me mah-jong and we spent pleasant afternoons in each other's company.

He had a non-Jewish housekeeper who came round each day with her granddaughter, a girl aged about twelve. The housekeeper was in love with Mr Weill and jealous of the time I spent with him. Without my knowledge, she asked Antje to tell me to stop seeing him. Antje obliged and said that Grandpa Weill had the flu and I shouldn't go to him. A while later, the housekeeper invited me for a cup of tea and admitted that he hadn't been ill at all and had kept on asking for me. When he'd asked her why I'd stopped coming, she'd told him that *I* had the flu.

After the war I found out where he lived in Leiden and paid him a visit. His housekeeper was there too, and had since become his wife, so that's at least one story with a happy ending. I also found out that the girl I thought was her granddaughter was really Grandpa Weill's granddaughter. She was in hiding with the housekeeper, and passing her off as her non-Jewish granddaughter enabled her to survive the war.

Antje Holthuis was a typical Dutch girl with short blonde hair and pale skin. She didn't much care for fancy clothes, but given we were in the middle of a war, there wasn't much to be had anyway. She was very easy-going. I remember when a pregnant woman who was staying with us for a couple of weeks complained that there was grit in the salad. Antje could have been angry at the woman's fussiness, given the circumstances other people found themselves in, but she simply said she'd wash it again. She was relaxed about most things, except when she had to give someone medical treatment, at which point she became particularly fastidious. As it happened, it was she who ended up delivering the baby of the woman who complained about the lettuce.

Mien Lubbe was a very different sort, much taller than Antje and me, and very thin, with dark-blonde hair almost down to her shoulders. Most of us had that same hairstyle.

Although I was enormously grateful to both women, I always had the feeling that Mien and I didn't quite click. Of course, this didn't get in the way of us working together for the resistance. I just wasn't friends with her the way I was with Antje, though I did remain in touch with both of them after the war. In the last year of the conflict, Antje and Mien hid several men in their attic to help them avoid forced labour. They used the metal pipes that ran between the downstairs corridor and the second floor to warn them in an emergency. They really were very brave women.

When I first went to live with Antje and Mien, they said nothing of their resistance work. A number of doctors from the hospital in Leiden would come round for dinner and (unbeknown to me) resistance meetings. These doctors were working to save Jewish people who were taken to the hospital having attempted suicide because of the new German anti-Jewish measures. Among their patients was my cousin Iessy (Isaac) van Frank, a twenty-five-year-old devout Jew who suffered so terribly under the oppressive regime that he tried to hang himself. After they saved him, these doctors found a hiding place for Iessy and his family, which included my uncles and aunts from Leiden, Iessy's sister Klaartje van Frank – the cousin whose clothes Mams had altered for me when I was little – and my cousin Carla. They all survived the war.

In the beginning, the doctors who came to see us talked about medical matters, but I began to notice that as soon as I got up to fetch something from the kitchen, which was some way off at the end of the hallway, they would start to talk about other things. One evening, when Antje had told the group that I could play chess, she said that one of their colleagues, a professor of medicine, would love to have a game with me. I said I wasn't particularly good, but they encouraged me to go anyway. A week later they'd set a date – so I started playing chess with him. One day they asked me to pass on a message to him about a meeting, and on subsequent occasions I was asked to let him know that Mr So-and-So felt much better today or Mr Such-and-Such wasn't doing so well and would the professor please visit him. I never gave it any further thought. They all seemed like genuine messages and I was happy to pass them on.

Much later, I realized that the messages were in code and that the professor, like the other doctors, was involved in the resistance. Bit by bit, the group started to talk more openly about their activities and shared all kinds of stories with me. For instance, one of the doctors, Els Mulheisen, told me one evening about a number of men in the resistance who had been arrested, and mentioned the name of one in particular – Joachim Simon, or Shushu.

Simon worked with the Westerweel Group and helped set

up escape routes to France, Spain and, in the end, Palestine. He had been arrested when he crossed the border into the Netherlands after assisting a group of refugees to safety. He was imprisoned in the detention centre in Breda, where he committed suicide by jumping from a third-floor window, driven by the fear that he would succumb to torture and let information slip. After the war, a number of German war criminals were detained in the same prison, among them the group known as the Breda Three. Later on, I was to experience a run-in with one of the three, Willy Lages, the German head of the *Sicherheitsdienst* in Amsterdam, who had led the raid on the fur factory where I'd worked.

Els also told me that the resistance movement was short of people, especially young women. 'Is there any way I can help?' I asked.

The movement had helped Mams and Clara, and in return I wanted to do something for all those people who were taking such enormous risks to save others. Bob Jesse took me aside and told me in private that it would be extremely dangerous because I was Jewish, but I replied that I was used to passing as non-Jewish and was very keen to contribute. And, quite simply, that's how my courier work for the resistance began. The other members weren't told that I was Jewish – it was safer for all of us that way.

In fact, there were lots of Jews working alongside non-Jews in the resistance – many more than we knew of during the war. People often thought that the majority of Jews who escaped the deportations to the concentration camps immediately went into hiding, but that wasn't always the case. The fact that it wasn't in the interests of the Jews to be identified as such explains to some extent why so few were recognized for their contributions. The prevailing anti-Semitism after the war also played a part in minimizing the role of Jewish people in underground activities. People now think that the Jewish contribution to the resistance was very high relative to the size of the Jewish population before the war, so I wasn't the only Jewish woman determined to help. Very brave people took enormous risks and I too wanted to do whatever I could.

There were a number of different resistance groups in operation that had no contact with one another unless it was absolutely necessary. Each group concentrated on separate activities, which varied from providing bicycles and arranging train tickets, to producing false identity documents for people who needed help escaping and finding addresses for those going into hiding. Some groups were involved in sabotage, while others gathered intelligence.

I was part of a small subgroup consisting of Bob, who was known in the resistance as Peter Vos and was the group's leader, Jan Kraayenhof de Leur, a kind young man about my age who also came from Alkmaar, and me. We worked with the Catholics in the south, resistance groups in Friesland and Gelderland, and with the LO, the *Landelijke Organisatie voor Hulp aan Onderduikers* (National Organization for Help to People in Hiding). You were a small cog in a huge machine, and nobody knew exactly what anyone else was up to.

My role was that of a courier, which was useful for the resistance because the Germans were far less suspicious of young women. I would travel all over the Netherlands and cross the border to Belgium and France with suitcases full of illegal newsletters, pamphlets about strikes, money and food stamps for people in hiding, and false identity cards. The cards were not only for Jews in hiding but also for Christian youths who had refused to sign the oath of loyalty or had been summoned for transport to work camps and didn't want to go.

Working for the resistance might sound scary and exciting, and of course it was, but at the same time it all came to seem normal. Everything I did was dangerous, but the tasks I had to carry out were ordinary, everyday activities – taking the train, travelling with a bag or suitcase, delivering papers to people. It really did become routine, and in the end it felt like any other job. I did it so often that it became a way of life, just like modelling garments for Mr Mittwoch each day in the clothes shops.

In fact, the most remarkable thing was that most of the time I barely gave a thought to my safety. I wanted to help, whatever the cost – that feeling was very strong. You can't live in constant fear. Even fear is something to which you become accustomed. You have to set it aside and simply get on with what you are doing. Every day I did things that put my life at risk, but the acts themselves were no different from what I'd usually do as I went about my normal daily business. That's not to say I wasn't scared, but I didn't allow the fear to overwhelm me – the desire to thwart the Nazis and help people in danger was stronger.

A couple of days after I had said that I wanted to be involved in resistance work, Ann and Wim asked me to carry out my first mission. It turned out to be a terrifying task. Ann gave me a suitcase of papers at Amsterdam Central Station to be delivered to five different cities: Leiden, Dordrecht, 's-Hertogenbosch, Maastricht and Eindhoven.

When I got off the train in Leiden and turned to leave the platform I was nervous: most stations had control posts. I saw there was one there, manned by two German and two Dutch officers. They stopped me.

'What's in the suitcase?' one of them asked.

'Papers,' I replied.

'Open it.'

My heart was pounding. I began to fiddle with the locks, which I didn't know how to operate, and I was sure I would give myself away. In the end I got the case open, but I had no idea what I would find inside. There were five packages wrapped in brown paper with the letters L, D, H, M and E on them. I thought I'd had it then, but to my astonishment one of the German officers said it was fine and I could go. I walked away as fast as I could – careful not to look like I was making a run for it.

Once outside the station I began to tremble uncontrollably and developed a dreadful stomach ache. This pain was to become a physical manifestation of my fear, and in the coming months I would suffer from it often. When I arrived home, Antje and Mien said I'd gone green, and they asked what had happened. Mien gave me a stiff drink, which was certainly what I needed. The next day I successfully completed the task.

Another time Ann met me at Amsterdam Central Station with a gigantic suitcase. She put it in the luggage net across from my seat so that I could keep an eye on it but also deny that it was mine if necessary. A woman sat down opposite me and smiled. We chatted a little. The train stopped at various stations, and after The Hague I needed the toilet.

When I returned I thought I was sitting in the wrong carriage: the suitcase was nowhere to be seen, but the woman was still there, so it must have been the right one. Where in God's name had the case gone? Someone must have stolen it, but because I didn't want to attract attention, I couldn't ask the woman if she'd seen anything. I tried not to make it obvious I was looking for the suitcase, but the woman noticed my confusion.

'Have you lost your suitcase?' she asked.

'Oh, no,' I said hastily, but I must have looked miserable – it was clear she didn't believe me.

When we stopped in Rotterdam she poked her head through the window and called the conductor. 'This girl's suitcase has been stolen!'

Of course she only wanted to help, but I could have strangled her! A German officer came over to me.

'*Raus!*' he said, ordering me off the train.

I quickly prayed that the suitcase hadn't been found. On the platform he asked me where I'd put the case and what was in it. I said the first thing that came to mind: 'Underwear.' And because that sounded a bit strange, I hastily added, 'And other clothes too.'

The chief conductor blew his whistle and shouted, 'Close the doors!'

My train began to move off. Fortunately, the German officer was called away.

'Wait here!' he said to me, but as soon as he had his back to me I made a run for it and jumped on to the moving train.

When we arrived in Dordrecht, where I was due to change trains for Maastricht, I was about to get off when the conductor stopped me and asked, 'Are you the girl who lost her suitcase? What was in it?'

Once again I told him it contained underwear and other clothes. He gave me a small suitcase that wasn't mine and asked, 'Is that it?'

He opened it and it was full of clothes.

'Yes,' I said, desperately hoping to get away. 'That's it. Thank you.'

And I left with someone else's wardrobe.

In Dordrecht I went to the post office and sent Ann a coded telegram to her brother's address, telling her that something had gone wrong with the papers. Then I returned to Leiden.

Ann came round the next day and laughed at my story. She reckoned someone had stolen the suitcase because they thought it was full of clothes. She said it would be best for me to stay indoors for a while, in case the police or Gestapo published my story and photo.

Later, we heard that the suitcase had been found in a ditch, and we suspected that the papers were still in it, soaked through. We were very amused to picture how shocked the person who'd stolen the case must have been when they opened it and realized what a dangerous thing it was with all those illegal papers inside.

It wasn't my only brush with danger. There was one evening when someone rang our doorbell after eight. The curfew was in force from eight o'clock, so if anyone rang the bell after then it was always worrying – no one was allowed out after that time. Antje peered out cautiously from behind the curtains and saw a car with men in it from the *Sicherheitsdienst*.

Lies and I rushed to Mien's bedroom immediately. There was a small hiding space there, above the double wardrobe. We took out a plank and crept into the narrow gap. It was very cramped: with our knees pulled up and our heads tucked down, in the foetal position, we just fitted inside. Lies was above one side of the cupboard and I was above the other.

Fortunately, I was short and slim. I kept completely silent and didn't move a muscle, even when my legs went to sleep and my neck became so stiff it felt broken. I was genuinely terrified. In order to keep going I tried imagining it was all a game, that we were children playing hide-and-seek.

Meanwhile, clever Mien had quickly come up with a plan and removed all her clothes. When the German officer came in he was so embarrassed by her nakedness that he took only a cursory look around the room before going back out again. I have no idea where Grandpa Weill hid, but we were all safe.

By the time Mien said that we could come out again, I'd lost all remaining feeling in my neck and legs but I was extremely relieved. I don't know if I'd have been able to keep it up much longer. Mien placed a chair beside the wardrobe and helped us down. We could barely straighten our legs, but it had been a successful hiding place and we were pleased that we now knew we could stay there for a while. Nevertheless, if Mien hadn't had such presence of mind, things might have turned out differently.

Our house was owned by our neighbour, Mrs Christiaansen, and she also owned the one next door. There were two boys hiding at her place. I didn't know that one of them was Jewish – Mrs Christiaansen introduced him to me as her nephew. The other was Wil, a Catholic boy from Gelderland. Wil and I got to know each other one day when we poked our heads out of the window and started talking.

He'd refused to sign the oath of loyalty to the new German authorities, which was compulsory for students who wanted to go to university. As a result, he was summoned to go to a work camp, but he'd gone into hiding instead. We soon became friends.

Once, when I was visiting the house next door, a photo was taken of me in the garden with the boys and Mrs Christiaansen's two sons. We didn't stop to think how imprudent this was. Years later, my cousin Carla showed me a book about wartime Leiden and I suddenly came across that photo. For a moment it transported me back to Mrs Christiaansen's garden. I read the caption – all the boys were named, but I was 'an unknown woman in hiding'.

Wil often came round to our place. He and I would lie on the rug on the attic floor, listening to a radio broadcast from the BBC in London, ignoring the fact that this was prohibited. It wasn't long before we fell in love. If we weren't listening to the radio, we were kissing. There was enough time for that during the long, boring days when I wasn't travelling for the resistance. He was my first boyfriend and I enjoyed our time together to the full, until one day his mother turned up on the doorstep unexpectedly, with a girl who, it transpired, was his fiancée.

Perhaps Mrs Christiaansen had told his family that we had something going and they'd come to demonstrate that he was taken. I was devastated, and furious with him – he'd never mentioned a girlfriend, let alone a fiancée. I was cold towards him after that, but there was still something between us and gradually we grew close again. We were young and there was nothing else to fill the time, so it wasn't so surprising, but when I moved to Utrecht that put an end to it. Although he was my first love, we had no future together, and in the end my feelings for him weren't deep enough to keep me in Leiden.

One day Wim asked me to do something for him. He'd helped my cousin Zetty go into hiding in Leiden. She was alone. Her husband, Emile, had been an officer in the Dutch army and had fought at the German border at the time of the Dutch surrender. At first, he was sent home, but a number of officers were then rounded up to serve as hostages. The Jewish soldiers were separated from the others and sent to their deaths at concentration camps, mainly Auschwitz. Emile never returned.

Zetty and Emile's baby, Evalientje, who was born on 15 April 1942, was placed with a foster family. Rumour has it that she was left abandoned at the door of a couple in Oegstgeest, to the northwest of Leiden.

Evalientje began to see her foster mother as her real mother and always continued to do so; they were such formative years that she spent with them. The couple also had two sons and Evalientje considered them her brothers. It was very difficult for her to return to Zetty after the war. Not only was she emotionally attached to her foster mother, but she also had to leave a fairly affluent life for one of poverty – Zetty had little money.

Later on, Zetty also realized that it had been a mistake to send Evalientje to a Jewish school where all the children had lost their parents during the war. That's a distressing situation for a child.

Regrettably, mother and daughter were never able to build a normal loving relationship after their separation. This often happened to Jewish children who were rescued by non-Jewish foster parents and came to love them instead of their own families. Sometimes they stayed with their foster parents after the war, to the great sadness of their biological parents; other times they returned home, as Evalientje did, but they were never truly happy there.

Of course, there were also lots of children whose parents never came back and who were adopted by their foster parents after the war. That happened to the children of Zetty's brother David and sister-in-law Riekie, whom I mentioned before: Jannie, Levi and George.

In any case, Wim wanted me to go to Evalientje's foster parents, who were a very kind and pleasant couple, get a photo of the baby and then visit Zetty. Zetty and I were really happy to see each other, and she was delighted with the photo and stories I was able to tell her about her little daughter.

Zetty herself was in hiding with a woman whose husband was also an officer in the Dutch army and who had been taken prisoner like Emile. However, because he wasn't Jewish, this man was imprisoned in Germany rather than sent to a camp.

The woman needed the money she received for taking Zetty in, but she wasn't a kind person. She forbade Zetty from leaving her room, so the poor thing was locked up for months on end without anyone to talk to, apart from the odd word when the woman brought her some food. When the mother-in-law came to visit, Zetty wasn't allowed to move in case she heard something and started asking questions. Apparently, the mother-in-law had something against Jews. These circumstances were incredibly unpleasant, but people offering a hiding place had to take care not to be discovered and arrested themselves.

That wasn't the only time I went to see Zetty – I often visited her. I'd been trying to do some schoolwork, to keep up my knowledge and improve my languages and maths. When Zetty heard this, she offered to help me. We spent a great many hours studying English, French and maths together. I borrowed books from the same professor with whom I played chess and continued to pass on the clandestine messages.

This was a relatively good time for us, but it came to an end when the husband of the woman with whom Zetty was hiding was released and returned home. Now that her son was back, the mother-in-law visited more frequently and Zetty's presence was deemed too risky, so she was moved to a different location in Utrecht. It was to be a while before I would see her again.

After I'd carried out a number of missions for Wim and Ann, Bob Jesse became my point of contact. He was a sweet man who liked to talk, and a born organizer. He worked day and night for the resistance. He was very precise and had beautiful handwriting in which he carefully noted all kinds of details in his agenda so that he wouldn't forget anything. When he had

an assignment for me, he would come round with instruc-
tions, one assignment each time. Sometimes I was asked to
take documents, sometimes money. On some occasions I
went out with an envelope containing thousands of guilders
hidden in my clothes.

Bob often asked me to go to Haarlem – to Frans and Henny
Gerritsen's house. Frans falsified passports and identity papers
for people who wanted to escape. The resistance movement
obtained the documents that served as their basis in various
ways. Some were stolen from town halls or from individuals,
and some people who supported our cause actually gave us
their documents and told the authorities they'd lost them.
Others, who wanted to earn money, offered their papers for
sale. A number of officials who were on our side supplied us
with blank identity cards and ration books. The photos on the
cards had to be replaced, of course.

Initially, this falsifying of documents was done in a rather
primitive manner, but Frans Gerritsen was an artist and had
worked as a designer. Before the war he lived on Amstellaan in
Amsterdam, a couple of houses down from Bob and Dientje.
They'd become friends and Bob had asked Frans to use his
artistic skills to put the German stamp on the new photos. He
was exceptionally good at it and that was how he became
involved in the resistance.

Frans and Henny had also taken in a German refugee,
Paula Kaufman. She was very dark and looked extremely
Jewish, so it wasn't safe for her to open the door if the bell
rang, or to go out and do the shopping. Because Frans lived
so dangerously, he'd sent Henny and their newborn twins to

her parents in Zeist for their safety. To help them out, I was asked to go and stay for a while, to run errands and answer the door if anyone rang, while Paula kept house and cooked. She also helped process identity cards. She very carefully soaked off the old photo and stuck on a new one as accurately as possible. Frans would then draw on the requisite stamp. In the end, Paula also became very good at drawing those stamps. I learned too, but wasn't anywhere near as precise as Paula.

I often went 'home' to Leiden to sleep, but sometimes I stayed in Haarlem, especially when there were resistance meetings – with the Westerweel Group, for instance, where Bob, Jan Kraayenhof de Leur and I worked together. Joop Westerweel and his wife, Wil, were pacifist socialists and teachers at De Werkplaats, the progressive Kees Boeke school in Bilthoven, where Frans had also taught art for a while.

Joop and Wil had four children, but they still risked taking Jewish people into hiding. They'd become involved with a group of German refugees, young Zionist boys and girls who had come to the Netherlands before the war to study agriculture in preparation for living in Israel. That was how they'd met Paula Kaufman, who was also in the group.

Along with his colleagues, Joop organized an escape route through Belgium and France to neutral Switzerland, or to Spain, and eventually Palestine, and he saved two hundred and fifty Jews that way. He was arrested when he crossed the Belgian border with a group of Jewish refugees in March 1944, and he was executed in Camp Vught in August the same year. Despite being tortured he refused to betray his network.

Wil was also arrested and sent to Vught – she was even there when I was – and saw her husband again before he was executed, knowing it would happen. On the morning of Joop's execution he wrote a poem, the penultimate verse of which has become famous:

> If I go up or under
> it's not worth any strife.
> I feel the sacred wonder,
> know the richness of this life.

I often wonder how people were able to withstand situations in which their survival instinct had to take priority over true grief, but there was no choice. Wil was transported to Ravensbrück with our group in September, and we shared a bunk bed there. After the war she returned to the Netherlands. A large forest in Israel was dedicated to the memory of Joop Westerweel, in recognition of his work, and one of the trees in that forest was planted in my name, which was a great honour.

Meetings with this group often went on deep into the night. A number of people would stay over in Haarlem because the eight o'clock curfew applied to everyone, unless they had an *Ausweis* – a document that gave them permission to be out and about. The resistance had succeeded in obtaining such a pass for me, but I didn't want to attract attention by walking around in the street alone at night – unless there really was no other option. Frans and Paula slept in their own rooms, and Bob and Dientje slept in the guest bed. Everyone else, including myself and Coert Reilinger – a fellow resistance fighter I was to meet again after the war – slept on cushions on the floor.

One evening, while we were holding a meeting with around twelve people, the doorbell rang. Frans, Paula and I hurriedly bundled the tablecloth, with all the plates, cups and cutlery on it, into a cupboard. Everyone rushed upstairs to hide in various bedrooms and wardrobes. After a couple of minutes, Frans opened the door. It was the air raid protection officer, who thought he'd seen some light, but he must have been mistaken – Frans was very good with blackout curtains. Frans knew the officer, because they were neighbours, and had told me that the man was a Nazi sympathizer. We realized that we had to be extremely cautious and left the following morning at carefully planned intervals.

Whenever we went home, we made sure to do so before eight. Sometimes Joop would ask me to accompany him to the station. He liked to be around people and was a really interesting character, but I was uncomfortable being seen with him because he dressed so eccentrically. He was short and stocky, and wore a long coat, a large hat and brown sandals. Sometimes he would even travel with fake papers in a *Wehrmacht* car and would try to convince German soldiers of his antifascist viewpoints. He stood out and I knew that was dangerous. I tried to disappear into the crowd and I was always relieved when we went our separate ways – he to his platform and I to mine.

Frans was often away on a great many dangerous missions for the resistance. He would break into police stations or Dutch concentration camps to rescue people who'd been arrested, and he stole papers, generally identity cards or ration books.

One day, while he was away infiltrating a detention centre, the doorbell rang after eight. I opened the door cautiously to a civilian officer in uniform.

'There's a light on upstairs,' he said, and darted past me up the stairs. Everything must have appeared to be in order, as he came back down again not long after and left. But Paula had been concealed in her room upstairs. She came downstairs, as white as a sheet, and said the ladder to the attic had been folded down and that the officer must have seen it.

'So?' I asked. 'What does it matter?'

She told me that there was a young man around the age of eighteen hiding up there. His name was Norbert Klein and he was a half-Jewish German refugee in the Westerweel Group. In 1943 he'd been arrested and detained by the *Sicherheitsdienst*, then locked up in the department for psychiatric patients at the Wilhelmina Gasthuis hospital. Frans had managed to free him from there by placing a ladder beneath a toilet window. After he'd helped Norbert escape, Frans had built him a little room behind the attic wall in the house in Haarlem, where he could lie flat.

It was unimaginable that I'd been going there for months and never known that Norbert was hiding in the attic. Paula must have been extremely careful and only taken him food when I was out doing the shopping. It was better not to know one another's secrets, in case we were caught and tortured. When the air raid protection officer showed up, Paula had just taken Norbert his meal. She and I discussed what we should do next, and in the morning we sent a telegram with a coded warning to Frans' in-laws.

The following evening someone knocked softly on the back window. It was Frans. He had already climbed onto the roof near Norbert's hiding place to see how he was. Norbert told him everything was fine. When we explained to Frans what had happened, he said that I should go back to Leiden for a couple of days to be on the safe side. He checked the blackout curtains but couldn't find any gaps in them. I think the air raid protection officer had probably seen light from the lamp in Norbert's hiding place shining through the roof, but Frans said that was impossible, as he'd covered everything properly.

After that incident, as a precaution, Norbert went to stay with Dientje in Amsterdam for a while. I saw him again a year later. By then, I was living in Utrecht and Dientje had suggested we spend a long weekend in her caravan near Arnhem. To my surprise, Norbert was there too. He'd been living in the village for some time and Dientje often visited him. It later transpired that he was in love with her. She'd suggested I come to the caravan in the hope that he would switch his affections to me, but he and I had no such feelings for each other.

Norbert survived the war, but became seriously unstable. He had been so psychologically damaged by his experiences that he had to spend the rest of his life in a care home in Amersfoort. Frans visited him regularly after the war. I went too. It was so sad to see him as he was, not knowing where he was or what was happening to him. By then, he was in his thirties and seemed to have full-on dementia. He lived for many more years. When he died, Frans, who had always remained good friends with him, arranged his funeral.

*

Norbert wasn't able to stand the strain of being constantly vigilant – he wasn't alone in that, of course. It was a terribly hard way to live. But I, fortunately, was strong – physically and mentally. I didn't know exactly what I was capable of, but I felt resilient enough – perhaps because my childhood had been something of a rollercoaster ride – to do more than just hide myself away. And once I started my resistance work, I found that not only could I do it, but I also wanted to do more.

There was one occasion when I had to deliver an envelope to a priest in Heerlen, all the way down in the south of the country. It was a long train journey, but everything went smoothly and I made it through the checkpoint without any problems.

After I left the station, I went on my way to the priest's house. As I approached, I saw a young man leave the property, an envelope protruding from his raincoat pocket. Could he also be a courier? I couldn't believe he'd be so reckless – the envelope was clearly visible and might arouse suspicion. I wondered anxiously whether the secret police might be watching the building.

I decided to remain on high alert and – instead of immediately visiting the house – to walk right to the end of the street before making my way back slowly. You never knew whose eyes might be on you. I was still afraid when I rang the doorbell. I handed over my envelope and left for Leiden as fast as I could. Being suspicious and on high alert had become a way of life.

On another occasion I was on my way to The Hague with food stamps and money. I eventually found the address I needed, after searching for a long time. It was a typical Dutch terraced house with large windows, pretty curtains, and flowerpots on the windowsill. I rang the doorbell and a friendly woman, presumably the owner, let me in.

Two small children – a boy and a girl – were playing with some toys on the living-room floor. They were very sweet and I wondered who they were. A second woman was in a chair, sewing – I thought she was probably their mother. She was blonde and didn't look Jewish at all. We chatted a bit about the weather and the news. I felt bad for the children. It was a lovely summer's day but they weren't allowed outside. Of course, I could never ask any questions and nor could the mother.

Much later, after the war, Bob or Wim told me the woman was married to a Jewish professor. He'd had to go into hiding, and because they were afraid the Germans would take the children, the whole family had to do the same. It's terrible to be forced to give up your normal life and have to replace it with constant vigilance. I've often wondered about the long-term effects it must have had on their lives.

I know so many adults – now in their eighties – who were children during that time and went into hiding. You might think that they didn't understand what was happening or why, but it's surprising how much they knew. Such experiences are so disruptive to a normal childhood and some of them have never recovered. It's something that affects you for the rest of your life.

Meanwhile, I couldn't help but think of my own family. Mams and Clara were still in hiding, and that cost money; the woman they were staying with had to be paid. I'd known all that time that they were somewhere in Eindhoven, but only when I went to live in Leiden and became involved in the resistance did Ann give me the address. She had regularly taken money to them there. Initially, this was the money Pa had left with the Jongeneels, but when that ran out the resistance took over the payments. When I joined the movement I was asked to take the ration books and money there myself so that I could see my mother and Clara again.

The first time I visited them must have been in February 1943, about four months after they went into hiding. It was wonderful to be together again and speak to them. We embraced. We talked about what was happening and recalled old memories. We didn't talk about the future. On my visits I slept with Mams in the double bed, while Clara slept in the same room in a single bed. Each time we said goodbye, we would kiss, give each other a big hug, and say, 'Stay well, be careful and see you next time.' We never knew if there would be a next time. We were fully aware that they or I could be discovered at any point. I continued to visit them every month. In the end the fourth time turned out to be the last.

Their landlady also took in an elderly Jewish man and gave him her son's room. The little boy must have had to sleep with his two sisters and their mother in their double bed from then on. The mother also received a visit every evening from a German soldier who was her lover. It bothered me a great deal, and I told Ann how very worried I was. Couldn't she find somewhere else for Mams and Clara? I asked.

Ann replied that it was too dangerous to move them. Impossible, even. At that point the SS was strictly controlling the station in Eindhoven and all routes out of town. In her view, it was actually safer if a German soldier was dropping by every evening – after all, it would never occur to anyone to ask any questions. I doubted that. I suspected that one of the three children who slept in their mother's bed would let something slip one day at school – children joke around, they say things without realizing – and I was terrified that Mams and Clara would be found out. But what could I do? I had to accept it.

It turned out that my fears were justified. At the end of June 1943, when Mams and Clara had been in Eindhoven for around nine months, I received a postcard from Dientje: *Fem and Clara seriously ill. Come to me.* I knew that was code for something bad has happened. I was completely beside myself. Mien went with me to see Dientje in Amsterdam because she didn't think I should go alone. When we arrived Dientje gave me a card from Mams in which she requested a toothbrush and toothpaste. It had been sent from Westerbork.

The card was probably just to let us know that they'd been taken there. In any case, I went to see Greet Brinkhuis, as she kept large rucksacks of emergency items that we'd prepared. I took some toothpaste and toothbrushes to Dientje and we sent them on to Westerbork. Sickened by the news and desperate with worry, I returned to Leiden. I was distraught and wept all night.

That was the last I heard from Mams or Clara. I later learned that they were immediately put on a train to Sobibor and murdered on arrival. The date of their death is recorded as 2 July 1943. My mother was fifty-three and Clara was just fifteen.

After the war I went back to the house in Eindhoven where they'd stayed, to talk to the woman who had hidden them. She'd been imprisoned for a couple of months in Vught as a punishment for taking in Jews. She said she was sure her husband, from whom she was divorced, had betrayed Mams and Clara. It was either him, or his lover, with whom he lived, she said.

By the time I arrived in Vught she had already left, which was lucky for me. Otherwise, she would have recognized me and might have betrayed my true identity. After the war, my brother Louis went to the police in Eindhoven and gave them the name of the man we suspected of betraying Mams and Clara. When they interrogated him, he denied having had anything to do with it. I believe it was more likely the children who let it slip – it's very easy for a child to say the wrong thing – but we'll never know.

I cried and cried for many nights after learning of Mams and Clara's deportation. The only way I could deal with my grief was to really throw myself into the resistance. They needed people who could think logically, and that was me. And so I offered myself up for more work. By then, I was travelling so frequently that they found me a room in Utrecht, which was centrally located and would make the journeys rather easier. So I left the house in Leiden.

Amsterdam had become too dangerous for Bob, and he also ended up in Utrecht, in a room not far from mine. I received a set amount of money from the resistance and, generally speaking, it was handed over by Bob. I used it to pay my landlady and for other expenses – I no longer had any money of my own. I tried to live as frugally as possible, always conscious of the fact that the resistance needed a lot of money for everyone in hiding.

One day in Utrecht, I saw my old school friend Mary

Rudolphus walking down the street with her mother. Her family had moved to Bilthoven and it had been a long time since we'd seen each other. It was a wonderful moment: an agonizing meeting in harsh circumstances between two people who had once known one another through and through. Neither of us had ever paid any attention to my Jewishness, but now we couldn't even say hello. Mary must have realized that. We walked so close to each other that our arms almost touched. I smiled a little, but walked on as if we were strangers.

I never saw Mary or her parents again. After the war, I visited Frans and Henny Gerritsen, who had moved to Bilthoven from Haarlem. When I was there I called Mary's mother. She told me that Mary was married and living with her husband in Spain. I never went back to Bilthoven after that. Frans and Henny split up and moved again, so there was no reason to return. I was so devastated by the chaotic situation in the Netherlands and by what had happened to my family that I was too bewildered to consider things properly and rekindle our friendship. Now I deeply regret not having made contact again. In recent years I've considered pursuing it, but by now everyone has probably died.

Not long after I moved to Utrecht, all Dutch citizens were required to pick up new distribution cards to obtain food. It was early December 1943. In the resistance, we all had false identities, but now the TD group – short for *Tweede Distributiestamkaart,* or second distribution identification card – had a new plan. They wanted to use the details of people who'd died in early infancy to sabotage the use of the distribution card. I was the guinea pig and the first to receive another person's identity.

From that point on, I was Margareta van der Kuit, or 'Marga'. Apparently, I was born on 21 October 1920 in Soest. I was given a new identity card and had to try to obtain a new distribution card and stamps for shoes and clothes with it. It was a nerve-wracking task, but everything went to plan. Not only did I have a new identity, but we also knew that the system worked for others. Together with Bob, Jan and a few other intermediaries – mostly officials at the town halls – we were able to help a great many people obtain new distribution cards this way.

As Margareta van der Kuit I was now sent to even more places. Sometimes my resistance work took me to Amsterdam, and if it was too late to go back to Utrecht, I would stay with Greet. We would sleep together in the box bed in her room. We talked and reminisced for hours on end, but I was careful not to tell her too much about my activities. I didn't want to endanger her or her parents. Greet was very good: she always called me Marga.

One day, Bob asked me to go to the countryside and visit a farmer and his wife who were concerned about the non-Jewish student they were hiding. The boy was one of the great many non-Jewish youths who had opted to go into hiding because they'd refused to sign the oath of loyalty to National Socialism. He was very nervous and Bob thought he might benefit from some female company. Perhaps it would help if I went to talk to him. I could combine it with taking the farmer and his wife money and food stamps.

After walking around lost for hours, I came across the boy

in the haystack where he slept. I don't know if it helped him but we chatted for a long time. He was probably just very lonely. People in hiding often went for weeks without having a real conversation with anyone.

During our encounter he pulled a large smock out of the hay with half a dozen pistols hidden in it. He wanted to give me one, a small elegant weapon with mother-of-pearl on the handle, but I didn't want it. Bob had always insisted we mustn't walk around with guns – if the Germans found them, they wouldn't hesitate to shoot us.

Since Zetty was now in hiding in Zeist, Wim asked me to visit her and let her know how her daughter was doing. Eva-lientje was almost two by that point, walking and talking. Zetty turned out to be staying just a short bus ride from me, so I went back to dropping in on her regularly with money and food stamps for her landlady. It was lovely to see her again and to be able to chat, but sadly I no longer had time to study languages and maths with her. I was too busy with courier work, travelling here, there and everywhere.

To get to where Zetty was staying, I would take a bus from the corner of Burgemeester Reigerslaan, where I was living. One day it was raining cats and dogs, and I took shelter in a porch while I waited for the bus. I'd put up the hood of my raincoat so you could see only a lock of my blonde hair, so I suspect I wasn't looking my best. Out of nowhere, a German officer appeared next to me and opened his large black umbrella above my head.

'It's so wet,' he said. 'Would you like to come and have a cup of tea with me? I live right there in the house across the road.'

I was surprised and a little apprehensive, but I replied very politely, 'No, thank you. I'm fine here.'

Just at that moment the bus arrived. The officer insisted on holding the umbrella above my head until I was well inside the bus. I was wary, but I smiled and thanked him.

The next time I took the bus he was standing there again, and once more he started talking to me. What was my name? Did I live around here? Would I like a cup of tea? This time I was a lot more worried and said, 'No, thank you. I don't have time.'

Fortunately, the bus came along to save me from further questions. I told Bob what had happened. I said there was no way I could go back to see Zetty – it was too dangerous to take that bus in case the officer found out where I lived and what I was doing. Bob couldn't help laughing. He said that the officer probably just fancied me and told me we should take advantage of that.

'Two of our boys are in prison,' he explained. 'They'll be shot if we don't save them. Try to get hold of some of this officer's papers. Then we can use them to enter the prison and get the boys out.'

I hesitated to begin with. It was far too dangerous. However, the next time I ran into the officer at the bus stop and he invited me for a cup of tea, I thought of those boys in prison, set aside my fears and accepted his offer. He did indeed live in a nice house opposite the bus stop. He told me his name was Hans, he came from Austria, and he'd been conscripted to the German army. He was unmarried and lived with his mother back in Austria.

At that point, a group of boys from the Hitler Youth went past singing. Hans closed the curtains. He made a scathing remark and mentioned that he'd been allocated the house after a poor Jewish family had been turned out of it. He pulled a face as if he felt bad about it, but whatever he said, I didn't trust him. It could just as easily be a ruse to win my confidence. Suspicion had become second nature to me.

We drank tea and talked about his mother in Austria. Nothing more happened and I couldn't see how I might be able to get my hands on his papers. He said he liked talking with me and that I was a very nice girl. He must have been at least forty, so I assume he considered himself lucky to have contact with such a young woman. He asked if I'd like to have tea with him again sometime, and with Bob's imprisoned boys in mind I said yes. My only hope was to win his trust and wait for the right moment.

We arranged to see each other again a couple of days later and I knocked on his door around four o'clock in the afternoon. After tea he suggested dancing and put on a record. We danced waltzes and foxtrots to the sentimental music. It was all rather strange and I still had no idea how I could get hold of his papers.

After a while, he pulled me over to the sofa and began to caress me. I let him do his thing, while I tried to keep a cool head and come up with a plan. The buttons and medals on his uniform were digging into me, so he took off his jacket and I wondered how far he thought this would go. Suddenly he asked me if I was a virgin. When I said yes, he stopped right away. I realized that he was a gentleman – kind and respectful – and

I felt bad for betraying him, but the boys in prison were my priority.

At that point, he suggested having a drink and went into the kitchen. I saw my chance and hastily searched his jacket, my heart pounding. I found a paper with a German stamp and a signature, and quickly stuffed it into my bag. When he came back I was sitting in my place, trying to look relaxed. My hands didn't shake. My breath didn't tremble. I chattered away as naturally as I could and hoped he would attribute any trace of nerves to the inexperience of a young woman. As soon as I could make my excuses, I left.

In the end, I felt sorry that I conned him. I was terrified he would notice what I'd done, but Bob assured me that even if he did he wouldn't say a word to his seniors. After all, it would make him look like an idiot and he'd be sent to the front in Eastern Europe. After the war I found out that he had indeed been sent east, but I don't know whether this had anything to do with the lost document. It may have been a while before he realized that it was missing, so he may have just thought he'd lost it. Nevertheless, in the months that followed I took good care not to go near his house or the bus stop again.

My most dangerous and longest mission was to Paris. I'd been assigned tasks involving travel to the south of the Netherlands before and had crossed the border into Belgium. I would get out at the station near the border, walk across the farmland into Belgium and stay in a farmhouse near by, where the farmer and his wife were known to the resistance and offered accommodation to people in hiding.

For someone who'd been outside the Netherlands only once before the war, on a school trip to England, I had become a seasoned traveller surprisingly quickly, but I'd never been to France. There were groups of Dutch resistance workers there, whose work included trying to open up new escape routes to the borders with Spain and Switzerland. Joachim Simon, or Shushu, whom I mentioned before, played an important role there.

Various Jews and non-Jews were successfully taken across the border, which often involved walking for days in France and hiking over the Pyrenees. Some of them travelled on to Portugal, including a number of people from the original Westerweel-Palestine Group who successfully continued their journey to what is now Israel.

In April 1944, however, a few resistance fighters who were connected with the Westerweel Group were arrested in Paris and held in Fresnes Prison in Val-de-Marne, south of Paris. There, British spies and people from the French resistance were detained in unspeakable conditions and tortured. If we couldn't get our boys out they would be murdered.

Bob and Frans asked me to go to Paris. I had to hand over an envelope to someone who worked in the German head-quarters; he would give me some papers to bring back. I didn't know how my task would contribute to the rescue attempt, but I was told it was essential. One thing was clear: this mission was extremely dangerous. I'd taken a great many risks already, but I'd never done anything as perilous as entering a German headquarters.

Filled with fear, I took the train south, crossed the border with the help of the farmers, travelled through Belgium, and then crossed the border into France. I had been given a different identity document to use in France if necessary, but I was terrified on the train and tried to avoid checks as far as possible.

Once in Paris I had no idea how I was to enter the German headquarters. As I approached the building, I could hear my own heart pounding. In hindsight it seems I was being reckless, but I knew what I was doing was crucial – and although I was extremely afraid, I knew I just had to do it. I've always had a lot of self-confidence, but I think on some level I no longer really cared about the danger. Of course I wanted to be safe, but I'd already lost so much that there wasn't much more at stake.

My strategy was to flirt with the soldiers outside and in the waiting room. Although I spoke German, I didn't want to enter into conversation and draw attention to myself. So I smiled and flirted silently, using my eyes, as if I was interested in the men. I tried to give the impression that I was having a great time. They responded to my gaze and gave me suggestive looks, so it was clear my plan was working.

At the reception I asked for my contact by simply giving his name, so as to talk as little as possible. Fortunately, he came quickly and we exchanged envelopes. Of course, he was taking a huge risk as well. I went back outside as quickly as I could and smiled at the soldiers on my way.

Everything went surprisingly smoothly; I'd expected a lot more security and questions. I assume it didn't occur to the

Germans that a young Jewish woman in the resistance would dare to enter their building, especially not acting as if she fancied them. To this day I cannot believe I got in and out so easily.

All the way back to the Netherlands I was careful. I changed clothes on the train in case anyone's suspicions had been aroused and a description of me had been circulated, and I made my way to the address I'd been given where I could hide. The farmer then took me across the border to Belgium. First, I walked on for several kilometres, then I took the tram as far as it went, and then the bus. I stayed the night with another farmer, near the border with Brabant, and the following day he took me across the border into the Netherlands. After another bus journey, I took the train to Roosendaal, changed trains, and after two long days of travel arrived back in Utrecht.

I handed Bob the envelope with a feeling of abject relief. I'd been so scared throughout the mission that I'd developed a bad stomach ache. At the time, I had no idea what effect, if any, my actions had had, but after the war I heard that the boys who had been arrested had survived. So my ordeal had been worth it.

6

Secret Drawers: *My arrest*

To carry out our work in the resistance, we needed the tools of a secret agent: fingerprint kits, equipment for attaching photos to identity cards, ink pads for stamping, ration cards, and so on. I kept these supplies in a case under my bed in my room in Utrecht, which was a risky thing to do.

Frans Gerritsen, the man who was very talented at design, had promised to make me some bookshelves with hidden drawers in them, so that I'd have a safer keeping place for these items. I'd been waiting for them for six months already, but Frans had been very busy, saving people from prisons, hospitals and Westerbork.

Finally, on 18 June 1944, not long after my twenty-second birthday, Jan phoned to say he had the shelves. He'd picked them up from Frans in Haarlem and wanted to show me how they worked. He told me he'd take them to Bob's house in Utrecht because it was closer to the station than mine was. When I thought about this later, I questioned the logic behind his reasoning – the shelves would have to be taken to my place in any case so that they could be screwed to the wall. But that didn't cross my mind at the time and I went to Bob's house without hesitation. Jan showed me a few times how to open the hidden drawers.

The landlady had set the table for lunch, so we assumed that Bob would be home at any moment. I'd just commented, 'Bob isn't back yet,' when we heard the front door open. 'Speak of the devil,' I said.

I opened the door to his apartment, looked down the staircase and, to my horror, saw Bob at the bottom, standing between two officers from the *Grüne Polizei*. In Germany, more and more of these regular police officers were being conscripted to the Nazi regime. They got their name from the green uniforms they wore. Ultimately, they were responsible for upholding Nazi laws.

They had been looking for Bob for a while when they spotted him on the train and arrested him. Bob hadn't expected us to be at his house and he blanched with shock when he saw us. All three of us stood paralysed for a moment, before I bolted upstairs in an attempt to escape. But there was no way out.

The *Grüne Polizei* officers came after me and dragged me downstairs. They started interrogating us: who were we and what were we doing there? They searched the room, opened up all the cupboards and drawers. In one of the cupboards, hidden behind some clothes, they found a gun. I felt the blood drain from my face. Bob had always forbidden us from carrying a firearm: if the Germans were to find it, they'd shoot you dead on the spot. What's more, our group had claimed we fought peacefully, without weapons. Perhaps that was naive, but we didn't want to operate on the same level as our oppressors. It was important to resist in ways that didn't rely on violence.

I was terrified, and not without reason. I said I was just a friend, which Bob and Jan confirmed – we'd agreed this strategy beforehand for this kind of eventuality. We didn't get a chance to talk further and weren't even allowed to look at one another. They dragged us out onto the street and took us to the prison in Utrecht in separate cars.

The two *Grüne Polizei* officers in the car with me were very large. I was sandwiched between them and could hardly breathe. It was desperately uncomfortable. I had no idea where we were going and the unknown is always frightening. However, I was mentally prepared for it; we all knew we were taking risks and that we could be arrested at any point. Because I had already considered the possibility that this would happen, I was able to focus on sticking to my story and acting innocent.

When we arrived at the prison in Utrecht, I was ordered to take a bath. All the prisoners had to take one on arrival – to keep us clean, but also to check we weren't hiding anything on our person. A friendly guard, an older lady in her forties or fifties, supervised me. She asked if I had a diary on me and when I said I did, she told me to dispose of it in the toilet. I told her there wasn't anything important in it, but she said they always found something, so I ripped it up into small pieces and flushed them all away.

Our paths crossed again in Ravensbrück, where she was being held prisoner, just like me. She was there because she and her brother had helped someone escape from prison. She was clearly a brave woman who had taken great risks. Unlike some people who took Jews into their homes, this lady wasn't paid for her efforts; she acted out of a genuine desire to protect people from the atrocities she saw around her. I regret to say she was murdered in Ravensbrück.

There was a big common room in the prison, which contained three cells with iron bars. After I'd had a bath, I was given some clothes and taken to the common room. There were two other girls there. The younger one had black circles under her eyes and her dark hair was a mess. The other, who was probably in her late twenties, was sitting calmly at the table, knitting. When she went to the toilet, the younger girl whispered to me that the other girl was an informer who was there to draw us out of our shells and get us to talk about what we had done. So I said, 'I haven't done anything. I'm just a friend of the boys they arrested.'

I stuck to that story the whole time, regardless of who I spoke to. I didn't dare trust even this young, sickly girl, although she was probably entirely innocent. The Nazis promised you everything if you betrayed others, and desperate people can be tempted to do almost anything if their lives depend on it.

A few hours later, the young girl was taken away to say goodbye to two friends who had been arrested at the same time as her. They were about to be executed. One of them was her boyfriend. The poor girl looked awful when she returned. She cried for hours on end. I tried to comfort her, but what comfort is there if you have just heard that the people you love are about to be murdered and you realize you've seen them for the last time.

She had also been sentenced to death at that trial. However,

I met her again in Sweden after the war, so they must have decided to let her live. She had gone on to be held as a *Nacht und Nebel* prisoner in various prisons in Germany before being liberated and sent to Sweden.

Hitler had introduced the *Nacht und Nebel* order for political activists and resistance fighters from the occupied countries on 7 December 1941. The idea behind the order was that these people would disappear without a trace. If they died, no record was made of their burial place, so as to intimidate the local population and deter them from working against the Nazis.

To this day, we don't know how many people vanished that way. After the war, many families were unable to work out what had happened to their loved ones. I wonder how long they spent hoping they would show up. Hardly any *Nacht und Nebel* prisoners survived the war. And those who did were treated in the most brutal ways during their imprisonment.

After spending a night locked up on my own in one of the three cells, my clothes were handed back to me and I was taken to Amsterdam in a small car with the two corpulent *Grüne Polizei* officers. Once again, I was squashed in between them. This time the experience was even worse because we stopped off at a butcher's on the way, where one of the men bought two huge German sausages. They scoffed them while I became more and more squashed between them. The smell of the sausages entered my nostrils and I could hear them chewing. I felt nauseated and feared I was going to be sick, but I didn't let it show. I breathed through my mouth instead of my nose and tried to appear calm.

Before long, we arrived at the large secondary school on Euterpestraat, which the *Sicherheitsdienst* had seized. It was using the building as its headquarters, and it's where they interrogated and tortured people. Because of its horrifying associations, the street was renamed Gerrit van der Veenstraat after the liberation, in honour of resistance hero Gerrit van der Veen. At the time, I couldn't have imagined any of that.

We got out of the car and found ourselves at the bottom of a tall stone staircase. At the top stood a man with a high forehead and dark, sunken eyes, in uniform and boots. I'd heard what happened to people who were arrested, so I was terribly afraid.

'What have we got here?' he asked.

'Oh, the girl has nothing to do with it,' the German man who accompanied me replied.

I immediately felt a flood of relief. But then the man said, 'I doubt that.'

My heart sank. Until that point I had always maintained that I was just a friend and didn't know what the others were up to, and I'd had the impression that the two *Grüne Polizei* officers believed me. Nevertheless, I smiled, and kept smiling. If I had known it was Willy Lages, the head of the *Sicherheitsdienst*, who was looking down at me from the top of the staircase, I don't know if I'd have been able to hold my smile. I only recognized him later, from his photos in the newspaper.

Once inside the building, I was told to go and sit in an easy chair. I had a bag with me that I'd crocheted from fisherman's rope. I'd made similar bags for friends' birthdays or for gifts for St Nicholas' Day. You couldn't get anything in the shops, so we made our own gifts with whatever material we could get our hands on. An official took away the bag and my papers to check them, and I froze with fear. I thought my final hour had come! It was one thing for a soldier or SS officer to check my papers on the train or platform, but an official check in the *Sicherheitsdienst* headquarters, where they probably had superior methods, was another thing entirely.

My all-too-familiar stomach pain resurfaced, but I kept smiling regardless. With feigned interest, I eyed up the uniformed girls sitting behind their desks, and the soldiers and SS officers who came and went. I looked around as if I hadn't a care in the world and nothing to hide.

By that point, I'd got used to assuming different roles. Ever since joining the resistance, I'd buried my true self. I consciously denied my essence – my 'Selma' – the whole time. I didn't dare think about anything related to my original identity in case I talked in my sleep and let slip my public mask of Margareta van der Kuit. I couldn't afford to relax. I had to be on guard the whole time so that I could respond if my adopted name was called, and so that I never accidentally replied 'Selma' when asked who I was. The officer eventually returned and gave me back my bag; it seemed that my papers were in order. Fortunately, the work of the resistance was up to scratch.

On 20 June, two days after my arrest, another car took me to the large prison on Amstelveenseweg, where all Jews and political prisoners were held while awaiting their deportation. They threw me into a cell with six other women. I was absolutely exhausted, but didn't dare sleep in case I talked. I kept drifting off and jerking myself awake again, so I paced around the cell in an attempt to stave off the tiredness. I spoke a bit with one of my cellmates during the night. We outlined, in broad terms, why we were there, but I was always careful about what I said and stuck to my cover story.

The facilities were very primitive, but at least the cell wasn't dirty and it didn't smell. In fact, the prisoners were given a bucket with water, soap and a piece of cloth, and we were expected to clean the space every day. In one corner was a second bucket that served as a toilet, which we had to put outside every morning. Then we were allowed to get a breath of fresh air in the courtyard in the middle of the prison; each cell had its own small area you could walk out into. I'd never been in a prison before and the rows of cells on the first floor looked intimidating. The other female prisoners and I weren't allowed to talk, but we did, of course. We were always pushing the boundaries. They'd tell us to stop talking, and so we would. For a while.

The male prisoners were kept a floor below us, and at one point I learned to tap on the pipes and listen to their tapped messages back. I wasn't particularly familiar with Morse code, but some people communicated very effectively with it. If you pushed your ear up against the pipes, you could also make out some whispering, catch a few words and fill in the gaps.

The cell opposite ours had a yellow Star of David on the door. It was clearly where the Jewish women were being held. I felt a deep sorrow for them, but at the same time I was anxious. I was scared to death that my Jewish identity would be discovered. I hardly dared even look at that door.

The first morning, after putting the bucket out, I was taken to another cell. Then the interrogations started. A German SS officer, the interrogator, sat behind a small table in a tiny room. There was a man standing behind him, and another behind me. The arrangement was intended to intimidate me. The interrogator asked if I understood German. 'No,' I said. I could actually speak it rather well, but denying it was an act of resistance. Everything German was cursed.

A Dutch man was brought in to go through the questions in the presence of the German officer and he started by asking my name.

'Margareta van der Kuit,' I replied.

Then he asked about the boys and what we were up to. I said I was just a friend and didn't know anything. He asked about my parents and I told him they'd been killed in a train accident before the war, while on holiday in England. I'd planned that story in advance. I tried to keep it all as simple and as convincing as possible, so that I'd be able to remember what I'd said. I hoped I wouldn't stray from this too much if I talked in my sleep.

I also told them my brothers were in England, which was actually true in David's case, at least as far as I knew, and it seemed sensible to stick to the truth wherever possible. But I didn't say that Louis had left with the merchant navy when the war broke out, or that David had been posted to England. After a great many questions, I was sent back to my cell.

There was just one bed in our cell, even though there were seven of us. One of the women was a farmer's wife who was very selfish and occupied the bed the whole time. She'd been taken prisoner because the SS were looking for her son. Sometimes family members were imprisoned in order to draw someone else in. Her husband hadn't been arrested because he was a farmer and his work was indispensable. He brought her food parcels from the farm, but even though prisoners got hardly anything to eat and the meagre amount we did get was foul, she never shared anything with us.

Another girl, a nurse about my age, had been imprisoned because she had refused to care for a German soldier. We sang Dutch folk songs together and did gymnastic exercises to stay fit. The farmer's wife complained about our activities, from her position on the bed. She told us to stop, but we ignored her, and kept singing tunes and marching around to try to keep our spirits up.

The cell was only a couple of metres from one wall to the other and we marched back and forth dozens of times, keeping count. I now realize that this must have been incredibly annoying for the other women because there was so little space, but we were young and energetic, and we didn't give it a second thought at the time. When the nurse was later released, she found Greet and told her that I, Marga, was in prison on Amstelveenseweg.

We did one another's hair so we would look as good as possible. One time, the young nurse was combing my hair, which had visible roots by then.

'You've got beautiful curls,' she said. 'Just like Jewish hair.'

I was terribly shaken, but I managed to laugh and said, 'Don't be ridiculous!'

One day, the guard took the nurse and me to her room to patch up socks and uniforms. We were scared that something was going to happen to us, but she started chatting. She said she'd taken us out of the cell so we could get a bit more air, have more freedom to move and for a bit of variety. We were grateful because the other women had started to get on our nerves with their never-ending moaning; they were probably just as happy to be rid of us for a few hours. We made sure we didn't say too much, though, because the guard seemed to ask a great many questions about our lives. You never knew who you could trust, we reminded each other.

I was interrogated every day for a week, but I wasn't treated roughly or manhandled. One time the interrogator asked why I had dyed my hair blonde, indicating my obvious dark roots.

'What else is a girl to do?' I replied. 'You can't buy clothes or shoes. The only thing you can do is your hair.'

He accepted that and let it go. Another day he offered me a cigarette and I shuddered as I recognized the packet from the case under my bed. I knew it was the same packet because I'd written the date on it, the way my father always did with the shopping. Of course, all the resistance tools and supplies had been in that case too. The interrogator said that Hitler didn't murder women, so I'd be best off telling him the truth. What was my work? What did I do?

I kept saying I was just a friend of Peter and Jan's. I don't know how I got away with it, considering the contents of the case, but he believed me. He probably thought it was Bob or Jan's case and it had been hidden there without my knowledge. I had to stay alert to make sure I kept referring to Bob by his resistance name, Peter, during the interrogations. I couldn't afford a slip of the tongue.

In the end I was sentenced to *Kriegsdauer* – imprisonment

for the duration of the war. It came as a relief; I was starting to realize that it was perhaps safer for me in the prison than outside. At least I knew what I could expect in there and I couldn't be arrested with my fake papers. What's more, I wasn't classed as a *Nacht und Nebel* prisoner. That would have been far more dangerous. The Germans were more interested in Bob and Jan than in me. I later found out that both men had been brutally mistreated during their interrogations.

About ten years ago, I went to the NIOD Institute for War, Holocaust and Genocide Studies in Amsterdam, where the official archives are kept. I wanted to know the exact date of my arrest and found out it was 18 June 1944. The archivist brought me all the files that mentioned my name – a huge pile – and I read about what had happened to Bob and Jan. Things I hadn't known before.

The SS had found Bob's diary, for instance. He was always very organized and had written down in it the date of an upcoming meeting in Limburg with the leaders of the resistance. It was a devastating oversight, but that's easy to say now. Bob was completely overworked because so few people were involved in the resistance, and the stress and long days had made him unwell. He'd stopped doing resistance work altogether for a couple of weeks, but that hadn't been enough time to recover. He was so exhausted that it would have taken far longer than that for him to get back to his usual self.

When he was interrogated, he refused, despite being beaten, to say where the meeting was being held – until a Jewish woman and her two small children were brought in. The interrogators held on to the arms of one of the children and threatened to break them if Bob didn't tell them the location of the meeting and take them there. Bob kept his lips sealed, but the terrified mother started screaming; she latched on to Bob and begged him to tell the truth.

The interrogator also said that Jan and I would be shot dead if Bob didn't give them the information. I'd heard the story about the child's arms before, but until I read it in the archive files, I never knew that they had threatened to kill me. In the end, Bob gave them the information. Afterwards, he said he'd had no choice.

Having revealed the location of the meeting, Bob was ordered by the SS officer to go there on the agreed date. He'd hoped he'd be able to escape or lead the SS officer the wrong way, but the SS officer who accompanied him was in plain-clothes. It was impossible. They told him again that Jan and I would be shot dead if he didn't go the right way. So Bob made his way to the convent in Weert where eleven resistance fighters, mainly leaders of groups in the south of the Netherlands, and a priest, had gathered.

The SS arrested almost everyone who was there. Four people escaped. The men who were arrested were all sent to concentration camps; only one of them survived. Bob was released because he'd helped the Germans. I knew nothing about this at the time because I was in prison, but when I was sent to Vught, Ada van den Bosch, who later married Wim Storm, told me what had gone on.

Ada had been in Vught previously, but had managed to escape and was free when all this happened to Bob. However, she was arrested a second time and sent back to Vught, where she was thrown into a punishment cell in the bunker. She had just been released from the bunker when I arrived at the camp. As she told me that the Germans had released Bob, she raised her eyebrows. The Germans only released people who had served them as traitors; her gesture suggested that that was perhaps also the case for Bob. I couldn't believe that Bob, who had worked for the resistance with so much courage and determination, would do such a thing. I said it couldn't be true, and Ada didn't take it any further.

However, this was all on the horizon. In the meantime, I was still in Amsterdam, living the life of a prisoner.

7

Blue Overalls: *Camp Vught*

My time in the Amsterdam prison came to an end on 26 July 1944. I was taken outside along with several other prisoners and we were marched to a tram by German and Dutch police. Passers-by looked at the procession of women as if we were a group of holidaymakers. The tram took us as far as the station, and from there we caught a regular train. We had no idea where we were being sent.

The women who welcomed us at the end of the journey were all political prisoners and they informed us that we'd arrived at the Dutch concentration camp in Vught. I didn't mind too much – they had me down as Margareta van der Kuit and, after the interrogations I'd had to endure in prison, I was sure it would be safer here.

It turned out I already knew a few people at the camp. Wil Westerweel was there, and Thea Boissevain, whom I knew about because her younger brother had been shot while he was working for the resistance. He was only seventeen. Ada van den Bosch was also there. She'd been sent back after her attempted escape, so together we formed our own little group. Resistance people tended to find one another in the camps.

Close friendships were absolutely essential in order to survive. You needed people who cared about you and who'd help you out if you got into trouble.

As soon as we arrived, we were made to shower. Our clothes, bags and other belongings were taken off us, stuffed into a sack and taken to a big barracks for storage. I'd managed to keep hold of my father's Waterman fountain pen until then but that went in the sack too, along with the blue cardigan Mams had knitted for my school trip to England a few years earlier.

After that, a doctor examined us. We were given blue overalls with buttons on the back that could be undone to allow us to go to the toilet, a blue headscarf with white circles on it, and a pair of clogs. We were meant to tie the headscarf under our chin, like a farmer's wife, but we later developed a more stylish way of wearing it by securing it at the back. That wasn't allowed, of course, but we did it regardless.

We were then taken to a barracks with lots of bunk beds, where we were given a blanket and allowed to get some rest. Two hundred and fifty people were housed in this big, barn-like structure. Each bunk bed was made up of two beds, and there were enough to go around – we could all sleep alone. There were plenty of windows for us to look out of. They didn't have any glass in them, so we could stick our heads outside – it wasn't like a prison.

The next day we had to line up for roll call to be counted. After that, we were put to work. I was given a bucket, brush, mop and cloth, and ordered to clean the nursery school. All the children who came to the camp with their parents attended the nursery – even the Jewish ones. Even those who were later sent to their deaths. When I got there, I was surprised to find men painting fairy-tale characters on the walls, and the prisoner who was also the nursery school teacher was openly flirting with them. There wasn't a guard in sight. This wasn't what I'd expected a camp to be like. It was typical of how the Germans ran things – they made things as normal as possible so that there wouldn't be any rebellions.

After a few days in Vught, I was sent to a gas mask factory in Den Bosch, not far from the camp. We slept in barracks there too, and each person had their own bed again. It was a luxury compared with what was to come, but I didn't know that then. We had to make gas masks for the Germans and most of us worked on the assembly line, each girl adding a part to the mask. An SS officer supervised us.

After I'd been working there for a few days, the girl opposite me, Hetty Voûte, told me I wasn't to tighten the screws too much, if I knew what she meant – nice and loose was the way to do it. The girl at the end of the line whose job was to check all the masks and put them in a wooden box turned a blind eye. She was part of the conspiracy too. In this way we sabotaged as many masks as we could. Thousands, probably.

In the sleeping quarters, there were five proper flush toilets. They were all very close together, though, and there weren't any curtains or partitions between them, so we didn't have any privacy. We were only allowed to go to the toilet at certain times, and there was always a long queue. One day, while I was waiting, the girl in front of me flushed, and the water tank came crashing down. I automatically leaped forward to catch it, breaking my thumb in the process. It bled profusely.

One of the prisoners who'd trained as a nurse found a small piece of wood and some strips of fabric. She made a splint for my thumb, bandaged up my hand and put my arm in a sling. I couldn't work on the assembly line with such an injury, so I was signed off for a week.

The weather was glorious, so I spent that week sunbathing. Looking back on this from the perspective of my later experiences in Ravensbrück, I can hardly believe it was allowed. Life in this camp wasn't so bad. While I was sunbathing, a couple of Jehovah's Witnesses – who had conscientious objections to the Nazis because they believed that Hitler was the Antichrist – came over and tried to convert me. I wasn't in the least bit interested. I just wanted to enjoy the sunshine.

A week later I had to return to the factory. I still wasn't able to work on the assembly line with my thumb bandaged up, so I was put in charge of checking the finished masks and putting them in the wooden boxes. By then, I knew that the women weren't doing their jobs properly, so I just gave the masks a fleeting glance and packed them up.

We weren't particularly worried about what we were doing. We didn't know what the consequences of our actions might be. Of course, we were all taking a big risk here. A woman called Friedl Burda was deported to Ravensbrück that same year, 1944, after spending seven months in prison for sabotaging weapons produced at the Reichert factory, which had originally manufactured ophthalmic instruments. She says in the *Ravensbrück Memorial Museum Guide*:

Afraid? Of course, we were well aware that we were putting our lives at risk. But it was worth it. I said to myself, 'It's better to give my life to a good cause than an evil one.' I can truly say I made the war a bit shorter. I think we all felt the same way about that. We had to do our bit to fight against these atrocities.

One day, a young woman arrived at the camp accompanied by an *Aufseherin* – a German guard. She told us her uncle was Karl Koch, who had been made commandant of Buchenwald in 1937. In 1941, Koch was re-assigned to Majdanek concentration camp in Poland in light of an investigation into allegations against him of corruption, fraud, drunkenness, sexual offences and murder. He even had a doctor and hospital attendant killed after they treated him for syphilis, for fear his secret might come out.

Koch commanded the Majdanek camp for only a year; after a group of Soviet prisoners of war escaped in August 1942, he was charged with criminal negligence and transferred to Berlin. His wife, Ilse, who later became known as 'the Witch of Buchenwald', stayed behind in Buchenwald. After the war she was given a life sentence for abusing and murdering German prisoners. A week before the Americans arrived in 1945, Karl Koch was executed for disgracing the SS.

Anyway, Koch's niece was engaged to a Jewish man, and she'd helped him go into hiding. As a punishment she was being made to visit all the camps to see what happened to people who helped Jews go into hiding – and that day she was visiting

131

Vught. She refused to go into the details of what she told us she'd seen. Perhaps it was better that way.

We knew there were some other work camps. In due course, some prisoners from Vught were sent on to a different camp, one other than Ravensbrück. At the time we thought there were a few of these work camps. In fact, there were thousands. We heard rumours, but we didn't believe them. Rumours were so often wrong. But there were no such rumours about extermination camps – we had no idea about extermination camps.

The next day Koch's niece left again with her *Aufseherin*. While it was comforting to know there was at least one German related to a high-ranking official who rejected the Nazi point of view, it was disconcerting to realize that even family members of the Nazis couldn't evade punishment by the regime.

Our working day in the gas mask factory started at six in the morning. We were allowed to use the toilet at noon. There was only one lavatory in the whole factory, so we spent a lot of time queuing up. After that, we had to go back to work again until six in the evening. We were only allowed to use the toilet again at the end of the day.

One evening when we were queuing up, three prisoners told me they were planning to escape and asked if I wanted to join them. The truth was I felt safer in the camp than outside, so I declined. I was scared to death I'd be caught again and they'd find out who I really was. So the prisoners asked for my help instead. Their plan was to sneak out through the toilet window, and they asked if I would close it behind them. I agreed and truly hoped their plan would work.

A few days later, we were rushed back from the factory to the camp. When we arrived, we were told that the Allies were close, in Belgium. We saw the tracer fire and bombs, and heard the planes overhead. We were thrilled at the prospect of being liberated soon. My joy was tempered somewhat when I also heard that my three friends had been caught within an hour of their escape. They'd cut through the meadow near the factory and had hoped to ask a farmer for help. However, at that very moment, one of the camp's German guards had been making out with a girl in the grass. He caught sight of my friends' blue overalls and clogs, arrested them and held them at gunpoint. They were taken back to the camp and thrown into a cell in the bunker.

The bunker was a punishment block. In it were tiny stone cells, each containing only a bucket and a small brick platform that was supposed to serve as a bed. It was almost always pitch-black in there. Scraps of food were pushed through a small hole in the door. There was no heating, and the prisoners were usually barefoot and wore just very thin clothing.

Such conditions were horrendous, but the bunker in Ravensbrück was much worse, I heard later. There, prisoners were tied to a block and beaten a certain number of times. They had to count the beatings, and if they floundered and lost count they had to start again from scratch. Few people left that bunker alive.

I was appalled by what the women in the punishment bunker had to go through. At the same time, I thanked my lucky stars that I'd followed my instincts and not gone with my friends. You always had to make snap decisions back then and it was so easy to make the wrong one. The three women never let on that I'd helped them, but we were all punished for their crime: we wouldn't be receiving any food packages from the Red Cross.

This was a joke because the Red Cross packages never reached us anyway. Before I arrived, people from the town of Vught and the surrounding villages had apparently sent in packages that actually reached the prisoners. But by the time I got there, that was a thing of the past. The SS guards and their families intercepted parcels and stuffed their faces with the contents. After the war, I found out that Bob and Dientje had been sending me food packages via the nuns in Vught. But they never reached me. I can just picture the SS guards tucking into them.

In retrospect, the conditions in Vught were relatively good. However, that's not to say that terrible things didn't happen there. My friends told me about a tragic event that took place in the bunker about six months before my arrival. In January 1944, a German prisoner betrayed some of her fellow prisoners, and the other women in the barracks responded by cutting off her hair. The leader of the barracks was then locked up in a cell. Ninety other women protested and signed a petition.

As punishment, the camp commandant locked up seventy-four women in cell 115: a stuffy space measuring just nine square metres. The women were squeezed in so tightly that the guards couldn't fit in the last sixteen and threw them into another cell instead. When the door of cell 115 was opened again the following day – fourteen hours later – ten of the women were dead and many others were unconscious. Resistance newspapers got wind of this atrocity and published an article. The commandant was dismissed and sent to the Eastern Front, where he died.

On the evening of 5 September 1944 we heard gunshots near the wall separating the women's camp from the men's camp. It was 'Mad Tuesday', when rumours that Breda had been liberated spread across the Netherlands, but that news hadn't reached us yet. About two hundred men – including the husbands and fiancés of many women in our part of the camp, some of whom I'd known in the resistance – were shot dead. The women had been taken to the men's camp to say goodbye to their loved ones. When they returned they were in a state of complete despair. We knew the men were going to be executed and did our best to console those poor women as they wept.

Hearing a mass execution take place is an experience beyond words. However, our ability to be shocked was perhaps less than it would have been under normal circumstances. After all, we'd already known people who'd been shot dead. We cried, but then we pulled ourselves together and got on with our daily lives.

8

The Passageway of Death: *Ravensbrück*

The day after these atrocities we were put on a train. That was when I wrote a letter on toilet paper to my friend Greet and pushed it through a gap in the wall of the cattle wagon; I hoped someone would find it and send it on. I addressed her as 'Gretchen' to try to be as inconspicuous as possible, and explained we were probably being transported to Ravensbrück or Sachsenhausen.

The journey took three long, exhausting days. Our destination turned out to be Ravensbrück. As we got off the train we were met by SS officers bearing whips, and dogs wearing the same uniforms as their masters. In the *Ravensbrück Memorial Museum Guide* you can read reports written by other prisoners who arrived there. Anna Stiegler describes how women who arrived in February 1940 were met by female guards with bloodhounds. 'Famished after the long journey and shivering from the cold, some people weren't able to march properly; they were shoved into the snow and intimidated by the dogs,' she writes.

Helena Kazimir, who arrived in November 1944, describes how 'The dogs were wearing exactly the same coats as their masters: military grey with an SS pin badge.'

Coming from Vught, we weren't used to the SS men with their whips and sticks hitting us. Pushing us. There was so much screaming and crying. But I didn't break down. Most of my group showed great self-control, despite the fear and uncertainty we felt. We walked towards the camp with as much dignity as possible. Keeping our heads up was another act of defiance. And we knew that if we cried or screamed there would be trouble. We didn't want to be struck if we could help it.

Ravensbrück was the only camp exclusively for women. Most inmates were political prisoners from France, Poland, Norway, Czechoslovakia, Belgium and the Netherlands, or German dissidents. Only fifteen to twenty per cent of the women were Jewish. Of course, I was there as a political prisoner, not as a Jew.

Nothing in Vught could have prepared me for Ravensbrück. There hadn't been many guards back there, and most of them had been Dutch. Some of them had treated us unkindly, but that was nothing compared with how we were treated now. Looking back on my time in Vught, it seemed like a holiday resort. We'd had food, showers, towels and proper toilets. I only realized how comfortable it had been, relatively speaking, when I arrived in Ravensbrück. I was pleased I wasn't there alone; there were women I knew from the resistance, such as Wil Westerweel, and from Camp Vught, such as Thea Boissevain, Gusta Eleveld and Ada van den Bosch. The only thing we could find comfort in was one another's company.

*

Ravensbrück is in an isolated location in northeast Germany, but easily accessible from Berlin. The first prisoners arrived on 18 May 1939. In total, one hundred and thirty-two thousand women and children were imprisoned there, of whom probably about ninety-two thousand died as a result of hunger, disease and executions. The cruelty was unimaginable.

In the early years of the camp's operation, newborn babies were taken from their mothers and drowned, or thrown into confined spaces to die. Many children were buried alive, poisoned or strangled, and hundreds of little girls were sterilized. Other children were forced to work, which usually killed them. Later, some newborn babies were allowed to live, but most still died as a result of the conditions.

As it became increasingly crowded, more than fifteen hundred people ended up living in barracks designed to house two hundred and fifty, with three or four to a bed. Thousands had to sleep on the ground, without even a blanket. Barbaric medical experiments were carried out on prisoners, and numerous women were sterilized.

Outside the Ravensbrück complex was a youth camp called Uckermark, which was originally built as a detention camp for 'asocial' girls and young women from Germany and Austria. The Nazis later used it as an extermination camp for women who were ill, no longer able to work or over the age of fifty-two. More than five thousand women were murdered there.

Women who had been given the death penalty were shot dead in the passageways between buildings, given lethal injections, or gassed in special buses that served as mobile gas chambers.

In 1943, the Nazis built a crematorium in Ravensbrück, and in autumn 1944 they built a gas chamber there.

The commandant's house was to one side of the entrance gate, and the sleeping quarters of the *Aufseherinnen*, whom we called 'mice' because of their grey uniforms, were just outside the main gate. These buildings still stand there today. The houses in which the SS officers lived were also outside the camp. The officers often led normal lives, with wives and children. They had well-kept gardens, maintained by German or Austrian prisoners who worked as servants or office staff.

The prisoners who did these jobs benefited from some food, fresh clothes and a shower every once in a while, and they slept in privileged barracks, which were also kept clean. The Germans were frightened to death of catching infections or lice, so they made sure the prisoners who worked in their houses were free from disease.

Red Cross employees who visited the camp only ever saw the privileged barracks, which created the impression that conditions weren't too bad. It only became clear just how terrible the camp really was much later on. The Siemens complex was on the hill above Ravensbrück. At first it was just a factory and the prisoners made their way there every day. However, a few months after we arrived, wooden sleeping barracks were built there for the Siemens workers.

Despite our frightening arrival, we didn't yet have any idea how awful the reality of life in Ravensbrück would be. The guards and their dogs marched us from the train to the camp, through an entrance gate in a big fence, above which *Arbeit macht frei* (work sets you free) was written in big letters. We walked past the guards and past the commandant's house to the main street, which was covered in ash and grit, before arriving at a tent. The ground inside was also covered in ash. This was where we'd be spending our first night.

We sat in the dirt and wondered what was going to happen to us. I tried not to think about where this might end up. Instead, I tried to focus on taking each day as it came. We were exhausted and all we wanted was to sleep. However horrific our circumstances were, that was the only thing that mattered.

'A creepy-crawly!' one of the women suddenly screamed.

It was a louse. Gusta Eleveld, whom I knew from Camp Vught, took charge. 'Everyone over to this side of the tent,' she instructed.

We didn't have a lot of space and slept pushed up against one another. This was quite funny in hindsight, because we'd soon be sleeping two or three to a narrow bunk bed and within a few weeks we'd all be covered in lice and wouldn't bat an eyelid. Half of our group spent that first night outside on the hill.

The next day we had to wait in a long queue to be *entlaust* (deloused). 'We don't have lice,' we said, but they screamed at us and shoved us into a building in groups of five, where we were ordered to undress. We were then pushed under ice-cold showers and beaten. There was always a rough hand on our lower back.

Afterwards, still naked, we had to line up so a doctor could perform intimate examinations on us. It was humiliating and degrading, and I often thought it must have been particularly terrible for nuns and other religious individuals.

The doctor didn't wash his hands and I don't think he wore any gloves. If he did, he didn't change them between examinations. I was furious that we were put at risk of infection. In view of the fact that some of the women were prostitutes, it's surprising that none of us ended up with a sexually transmitted disease.

We were then given a grey-striped prison dress, made out of thin material with a white cross on the back, but no underwear. We had to wear a red triangle on our sleeve to identify us as political prisoners, and the prostitutes had to wear a black one, designating them 'asocial' prisoners. We each wore a number on a strip of fabric on our left arm. Mine was 66947. Unlike in other concentration camps, the number wasn't tattooed on our skin.

When we went outside again, we bore no resemblance to the women in nice blue overalls who had stepped off the train and who had been referred to as *die schöne Holländerinnen* (the pretty Dutch girls). We looked like beggars. Some of the girls were crying – they'd had their heads shaved. They were told it was because of the lice, but I think it was done out of sheer cruelty because it mainly happened to those who'd had beautiful curls.

The first group who came out had warned us what was going to happen. The women from each group quickly passed on whatever valuable possessions they had, such as jumpers, to the next group so they could pick them up again later. Back when we knew we were going to be leaving Vught for Germany, Gusta had taken the blue cardigan Mams had knitted for me and my father's Waterman fountain pen out of the bag with

142

my belongings in it. She'd managed to smuggle the pen out in a thermometer tube.

She'd held on to these items since then, and gave them to me when she went into the wash hut. When it was my turn to go inside, I passed them on to others and collected them again when my ordeal was over. Being able to hold on to jumpers, shoes and other items turned out to be a godsend, because we weren't left with much after showering: just the thin prison dress. Some prisoners also had thin, striped cotton jackets. I took comfort in the fact that I still had my cardigan and my father's pen. Both items gave me a feeling my parents were near me, but the cardigan was also practical. I slipped my legs into the arms, pulled it up around my tummy and, worn as underwear, it kept me warm.

We were taken to the quarantine barracks, which were fitted out with bunk beds with straw mattresses covered with blue fabric. We were all exhausted and fell asleep almost immediately. We hung up our wash cloths and toothbrushes on the edge of our bunk beds, as we had done in Vught, but this was obviously very naive – by the following morning they had all gone. We later found out that the guards and prisoners referred to this as organized theft.

We were removed from quarantine the next day and the guards escorted us to our permanent barracks, where we stayed for a few weeks until we were transferred to the factories. There was just one entrance to each barracks. This was the *Stube* (day room), where the block *Älteste* (the woman who supervised the prisoners in each barracks) sat. This was usually a German or Austrian prisoner, or a criminal with privileges. She had a little stove she could use to boil water for coffee. She could also entertain her sidekicks – two assistant *Ältesten* – there. They were often extraordinarily inhumane women, beating their fellow prisoners with their fists or sticks.

There were about two hundred triple bunk beds in each barracks, so it was terribly overcrowded and the mattress covers were filthy. At this point I was assigned the bottom bunk, which was a good thing because I was having real issues with my bowels, and it was very difficult to climb out of the upper bunks if you were sick and needed to go to the toilet.

We were woken up at four every morning. Whatever the weather – be it rain, snow or frost – we had to line up for roll call in rows of ten. If we didn't get up quickly enough, the SS officers and the guards with German shepherds came and whipped us, screamed at us and beat us. Then the *Aufseherin* counted us and the SS officers checked the numbers. They never seemed to tally and every time they lost count they started again from scratch. When the numbers finally matched, we were sent away. Two women had to go with the guard to fetch a wooden barrel of watery substitute coffee, which we gulped down from our tin mugs. That was 'breakfast'.

In the evenings, after work and another roll call, we were given a ladle of so-called soup, which consisted of water with a few blades of grass or cabbage, along with a very thin slice of something that was meant to pass as bread. We joked that it was made from sawdust, but we gobbled it up nonetheless. We were always starving. We had to sit on our beds while we ate, with our heads bowed. Or sometimes we had to stand outside – there wasn't enough space in the day room for us all to stand there at the same time. What's more, it was safer to steer clear of the block *Älteste* and her assistants.

After a few days in the main camp, I was ordered to go and see the block *Älteste*. She asked me, with an *Aufseherin* beside her, if I wanted to go to a *Muttiheim*. She said I'd get something decent to eat and some milk there. I had no idea what a *Muttiheim* was. I knew that *Mutti* meant 'mother', but it all sounded rather risky to me. I declined, saying I'd rather stay with my friends. Surprisingly, you were allowed to say no. In any case, staying with my group seemed like the safer option. When I told this story to a few older friends, they started laughing. They told me that a *Muttiheim* was a place where girls were forced to have sex with German soldiers, so they would fall pregnant and have Aryan babies. They didn't know just how ironic that would have been in my case.

As the group of women were all political prisoners, we formed a unity. Even so, I never trusted anyone around me. As far as we could we looked out for one another, but I didn't reveal my true identity to anyone. All the time I stuck to my story – I was Marga.

Sometimes I'd hear stories about what some of the other women had done to be sent there – they had nothing to hide. But my cautiousness meant that people didn't trust me in return because I never talked about anything. It was just too dangerous.

In my first few days in the camp I saw a woman I recognized. She had been a rising star in the theatre: an actress, dancer and singer who had come to Amsterdam from Vienna. She was barely five feet tall, but she stood out with her fiery red hair. She had performed in the Hollandsche Schouwburg before the war and was becoming more and more famous.

I remember how I had really wanted to see her perform and started nagging my parents. At first, Pa said no – he was concerned that such outings weren't suitable for his nineteen-year-old daughter. He also thought it was an insult to go to the Jewish theatre, but I begged him until he eventually gave in. He, Mams and I went together in what must have been the winter of 1941, when the woman was only twenty-one. Despite her age, she attracted a dedicated audience. I can remember that evening well, because something in particular delighted me. Pa had an especially fierce laugh, and during the performance one of the actors on the stage said, 'I hear a familiar laugh!'

I was so proud that my father's colleagues recognized him by his laugh alone. And of course, the whole audience turned to him, which delighted me even more. When I saw that woman in Ravensbrück, I felt that my father was very close again. Even so, I did my best to steer clear of her – I was terrified that she would recognize me and unintentionally reveal my Jewish identity.

There were other pitfalls to watch out for in the camp. The other prisoners constantly warned us not to drink the water from the taps, regardless of how thirsty we were – it would make us very ill and could even kill us. Although I followed that advice, it wasn't long before I started to suffer from terrible diarrhoea. There was one morning when I couldn't get off the toilet quick enough for roll call. A German SS officer beat me with his belt, which was made from leather and metal. He forced me outside with it and I lost consciousness.

Two women carried me to the *Revier* – the sick barracks – where I stayed for a few days as I was very unwell. They deposited me at one end of a bottom bunk bed, even though there were already two German women at the other end. Even the sick barracks was crammed full. The next morning, those German women pushed me out of bed, screaming, 'The dirty Dutch girl hasn't washed.'

I crawled out the door to the corridor where there were a couple of sinks and taps, and I started washing myself, almost entirely naked. An older Polish woman who was standing beside me said, 'You Dutch women wash too much. That's why so many of you end up dead.'

An *Aufseherin* who was standing across the corridor heard the woman's words and looked up.

'Good grief,' she exclaimed, 'I thought the Dutch girl would be dead come morning.'

She pushed me back to my bed and, because she was there, the German women didn't dare say anything. I later found out that they had been imprisoned for trading on the black market.

After I'd spent four days in the sick barracks, some of my Dutch friends from the gas mask factory in Den Bosch came to the window to tell me they were being transported to another work camp and that I ought to go with them. But I was much too weak. What's more, I thought it would be safer to stay in Ravensbrück, especially since I didn't know whether the SS would scrutinize everyone's personal history again if we were transported. It was difficult to say goodbye to my friends. I had no idea whether I would ever see them again.

It was awfully cold, especially at night, even though we slept wearing all the clothes we had. I wondered if there was any way I could get my hands on some more layers. The chill certainly wasn't doing anything for my health. Someone told me about a Dutch mother with two young children who was working in the sewing block. Apparently she offered clothing in exchange for bread for her children. Although I was starving, I saved my small slice of bread for a few days and went looking for her.

From what people had said, I thought she might be one of Pa's acquaintances – he knew her husband. Although I had never met her, I prayed she wouldn't recognize me. If she did, she didn't say anything. I exchanged my bread for a pair of long johns she had stolen at work and was grateful for them – they kept me warm for the rest of my time in the camp.

Thirty years after the war, when I went to the unveiling of the Ravensbrück memorial at Amsterdam's Museumsplein, I saw my fellow prisoners for the first time since the liberation. I went up to Gusta Eleveld, who had become the chair of the Dutch Ravensbrück Committee.

'Do you remember me?' I asked.

'Of course I remember you, Marga. My bed was underneath yours in Ravensbrück. I'll never forget those white legs in long johns that would swing over the edge of my bed every day.'

I did my best to keep warm and strong. Our group of Dutch women had to carry out very hard physical work throughout the day, such as lugging heavy rocks from one place to another, digging big pits in the clay, or pulling a very heavy steamroller. Of course, the only purpose this served was to torture the prisoners. I did what I could to avoid it.

Wil Westerweel and I managed to sneak away to an empty barracks, where we crawled underneath the mattress of the highest bunk bed we could find and lay there, philosophizing about life. Because I hadn't had much experience with camp rules, I didn't realize just how dangerous this was – had we been found, we would have been beaten to death.

After a few days I started thinking about the risk we were taking, but then I was handed another way out. A friend told me that a group of Dutch women who had worked for Philips in Camp Vught were being sent to the Siemens factory, and she said that I should go with them. I'd never worked for Philips, I replied, but she told me that the Germans never looked at our details; they simply counted how many women went out through the gate.

I didn't need convincing any further and seized the opportunity the next day. There were hundreds of women in the queue and I joined them. I was afraid that what my friend had told me wasn't true, but everything went the way she had said. After the morning roll call, at about half past five, we went to the entrance gate of the camp. We marched up the long hill to the Siemens factory in rows of five and started work at six o'clock sharp. The Siemens managers were very strict when it came to punctuality. I later heard that they had to pay the heads of the SS only a couple of cents per hour for each prisoner.

When I arrived at Siemens I had to sit on a stool at a workbench. My task was to solder very fine metallic threads in small machines – I suspect they were aircraft components. I was incredibly nervous and knew I wouldn't be any good at such delicate work – I didn't have a very steady hand. I was petrified they would send me back to the camp, so every time a phone rang near by I would jump up to answer it and call over the boss, Herr Seefeld.

I hoped I would appear so useful that I would no longer have to work on the machines. My plan was going well, until the day someone important from Berlin phoned. I answered as usual and called over Herr Seefeld, but he was told that prisoners weren't allowed to answer the phone. That was the end of that, and I despaired. I became so nervous about messing up at work that one day I collapsed again and lost consciousness.

Although the stress couldn't have helped, I really was sick. I was so ill I could hardly think straight. I was taken to the sick barracks again, where they told me I had typhus. I was discharged after a few nights and sent to a nearby barracks, still in a weakened state. I had seen so many awful things happen that I knew I had to get better.

I knew, for example, that when someone called out for help – because she couldn't make it to the toilet herself, perhaps – the so-called nurses would take hold of the patient's mattress – one at the head, one at the foot – and throw her out of bed, even if she was in the top bunk. Under normal circumstances I wouldn't have been able to get out of bed at all, I was so unwell, but somehow I found the strength to keep going.

A Dutch girl with a yellow Star of David on her chest came up to me. 'Are you Marga van der Kuit?' she asked. She told me that Siemens was opening a new site that Herr Seefeld would be managing, and that he wanted me to go and work as his secretary. I never saw her again after that. I think she was sent to Auschwitz.

Once again, luck had been on my side – Herr Seefeld had noticed me answering the phone. Later, he also told me that I reminded him of his daughter. That fortunate coincidence, and my determination to walk out of the barracks and into the Siemens factory despite my weakened state, meant I ended up in one of the best possible positions in Ravensbrück. I sat opposite Herr Seefeld at his desk, during the day one week and at night the next. He was a big, very ordinary man in his late forties or early fifties, with a round, clean-shaven face and neatly combed-back hair. He'd worked for Siemens ever since leaving school. He was as friendly and humane as he could be in those appalling conditions, and we talked a lot, especially during the long, cold nights. My young *Aufseherin* wasn't bad either. I never heard or saw her doing anything cruel. She even let me go to the toilet outside the Siemens factory on my own, at night time too.

The toilet was in a small hut and was free-standing, like a portable toilet. On my solo trips to use it I thought a lot about possible ways of escaping, but you could see the watchtowers with their circling searchlights, and it seemed safer to stay put. I clearly remember going to the toilet a couple of months after arriving at the camp and finding the first louse on my body. Most of the women were already covered in them. I'd been afraid they might think my blood was different because I didn't have any lice, so I was extremely relieved when I saw that nasty creepy-crawly. How ridiculous! But my fear of being found out was certainly justified – most Jewish prisoners had already been sent to Auschwitz.

Typhus was not the only illness I was struck down with. I struggled with dysentery the whole time I was in Ravensbrück. The toilet block in the camp had channels in which you could relieve yourself, with taps above. It was quite a walk from our barracks. One night I had awful stomach pains and needed to use the toilet as a matter of urgency.

I was sleeping in the middle bunk and tried to hold it in while I climbed out of bed. I didn't want to soil my long johns and my warm blue cardigan. However, I couldn't manage any longer, and when I spotted a big barrel close to the exit to the barracks, I used that. The next morning, the block *Älteste*, who was rumoured to be an Austrian baroness, asked who was responsible. No one said anything. When she threatened to tell the *Aufseherin* and to punish the whole barracks, I confessed.

My punishment was a beating. The block *Älteste* hit me around my face and my head with her hands. It wasn't an option to fight back – that would have been too dangerous. When someone hits you, an automatic response to protect yourself kicks in, and my hands went up to my head. It didn't do much good. She beat me so brutally I lost consciousness and collapsed. My biggest fear was that she would inform the SS. She was a prisoner herself, of course, but she had power. Who knows, perhaps it was my job that helped to save me.

LEFT: *Letter from Selma to Greet Brinkhuis, written on the train from Camp Vught to Ravensbrück, 6 September 1944. The note was found and sent on by 'Mr Zoete'. Selma tried to find him after the war. Despite meeting many Zoetes, she was never able to thank him.*

ABOVE: *The letter's envelope, addressed to Miss Greet Brinkhuis.*

ABOVE: *Selma (bottom centre), Dit Kuyvenhoven (on Selma's left), Thea Boissevain (on Selma's right) and several Swedish acquaintances. Äppelviken, Sweden, 24 June 1945.*

BELOW: *First flight from Sweden to the Netherlands after the liberation. Dit Kuyvenhoven (second from left) and Wil Westerweel (sixth from left). Schiphol, summer 1945.*

VOORLOOPIG IDENTITEITSBEWIJS
CERTIFICAT D'IDENTITÉ PROVISOIRE   002080

De repatrieeringsafdeeling van de Nederlandsche Legatie
Le département de Répatriation de la Légation des Pays Bas

te Stockholm verklaart hiermede, dat de houder van dit
à Stockholm déclare par la présente, que le porteur de ce

bewijs identiek is met:
certificat est identique avec

Naam   Velleman   Voornamen   Selma
Nom   Prénoms

Plaats en datum van geboorte   Amsterdam, 7-6-1922.
Lieu et date de naissance

Woonplaats   Amsterdam.
Domicile

Kleur oogen
Couleur des yeux   marron clair

Kleur haar
Couleur des cheveux   blond moy.

Bizondere kenteekenen
Signes particuliers

Malmö   den
le

Repatrieeringsafdeeling der Nederlandsche Legatie
Département de Répatriation de la Légation des Pays Bas

Masterprint Fridman Sthlm

ABOVE: *Amsterdam Inspectorate for Repatriation document, August 1945.*
It reads: 'Selma Velleman. Amsterdam, 7-6-1922. Eye colour: light brown.
Hair colour: medium blond'.

LEFT: *David, Selma,*
Mr and Mrs Jongeneel.
(Mr Jongeneel was
the son of the family
David lodged with
during the first year of
the war.) Middelburg,
September 1945.

MINISTERIE VAN OORLOG

The Hague,6-11-1945

Movement Order

      You are ordered to
proceed by special military
aircraft from the Hague to
London on or about the..14..
of November 1945 and to report
for duty to the Neth. Ministry
of War, Arlingtonhouse, Arling-
tonstreet London S.W.1.

                    THE NETH. MINISTER
                         OF WAR,
                    for the Minister,
                  the Secretary General,

                    L.C.Rietveld.

   to
Miss S.Velleman passportno.427864.

*Selma is sent to London by order of the Minister of War and leaves on
14 November 1945.*

ABOVE: *Departing for London, 1945.*

BELOW: *Just arrived in London, 1945. Photo taken by brother Louis.*

LEFT: *Selma in London, 1949.*

RIGHT: *Playing tennis at Lincoln's Inn with two friends from the BBC (Selma centre). London, 17 April 1949.*

LEFT: *Selma and Hugo on their wedding day in London, 15 November 1955.*

RIGHT: *Selma at her graduation (heavily pregnant). London, May 1957.*

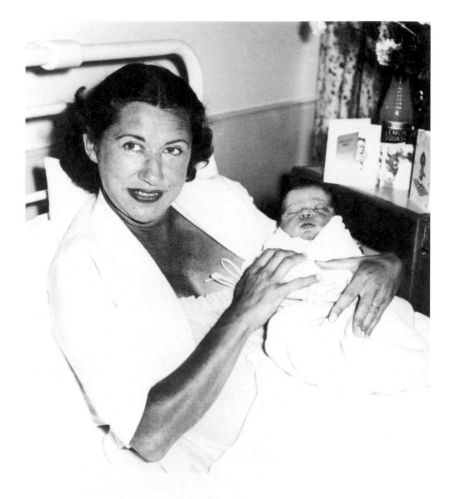

Selma in hospital with her newborn son Jocelin. London, 23 June 1957.

I wasn't to stay in those barracks for much longer. In November 1944, sleeping quarters were built for the Siemens employees at the factory. This meant we didn't have to spend thirty minutes walking to and from work every day. We also had the luxury of sleeping two people to a bed, instead of three or four. The women who worked day shifts slept there at night and the women who worked night shifts slept there during the day.

Apart from that, life was the same. Most of the Dutch women slept in the same barracks. We still had to get up early for roll call, and there was still that foul coffee and the work. One improvement was that there weren't usually any SS officers with dogs, just our own *Aufseherin* who accompanied us to the factory and stayed with us. We all tried to survive as best we could. Women who fell ill were taken to the *Revier* in the base camp, and most of them we never saw again. We were told they had succumbed to their illnesses, but we later heard they had been given lethal injections or been gassed.

We might have been only two to a bed now, but the conditions were still appalling. We couldn't wash our clothes, so the stench in the barracks was unbearable. It was almost better being outside at roll call, even if that sometimes meant standing in the freezing cold or snow for hours on end. Because we were all so weak and malnourished our periods stopped, but at least it was one less thing to worry about in those unhygienic conditions.

Many women were left infertile and doctors told me after the war that it was highly unlikely I'd ever be able to have children. There were other women, such as Annie Hendricks, who were already pregnant when they arrived in Ravensbrück. Annie's husband had been shot dead in Vught before we left. In exchange for some extra food – mashed potato and carrots, or thick soup with kohlrabi and carrots – she was doing additional heavy work, such as lugging large pots of soup, coffee or rubbish around after working all day or night. She had to do it herself; no one was allowed to help.

It was a wonder her pregnancy progressed as it did. We felt helpless but did our best to support her. As her child's birth approached, I offered to help in any way possible. It was a fair walk to the kitchen to collect the extra food she'd earned, and she had to stand in a long queue before being served, so she asked me to collect it for her. She gave me her voucher and I went in her place. I'll never forget the smell of mashed potato with carrots. For someone who was starving, that smell was mouth-watering. I must admit I was often tempted to have a taste, but I never did. Annie's son was born not long after.

The only time I got a bit of mash was when I almost died of dysentery and eventually went to the doctor. You only ever did that as a last resort. The camp was extremely overcrowded when we arrived and it was common knowledge that sick people were murdered. The doctor rarely showed up anyway, but if he sent you to the *Revier* in the main camp, you would be terrified that you would never return or that they'd use you for medical experiments before gassing you.

I became sicker and weaker because I couldn't keep down any food. I stuck it out for as long as I could, but one Sunday I gave in and went to the doctor's hut. Sunday was the only day you could go because you weren't allowed to take time off work. A new female doctor had replaced the male SS officer, so that gave me a bit of hope. I had to wait outside in the queue for an hour before I finally got to see her.

She was kind enough and gave me a voucher to get some mash from the kitchen. It was just one voucher, but it was enough to put an end to the severe diarrhoea – at least for a while. It never went away completely and I had bowel problems for years, even after the war. Doctors said my intestines were bright red, as if they had been inflamed for a long time. Even now, more than seventy years later, my bowels act up if I have a cold or I'm very run down.

Everyone had a tin mug, a tin plate and a tin spoon, which you had to keep on you at all times so they wouldn't be stolen. One of the women at Siemens, Tine van Yperen, worked on a machine where she had to nickel-plate wire, and she offered to use it to revamp our tin spoons. They looked wonderful afterwards, like real silver.

This may seem terribly unimportant, but we had nothing of any beauty – so if there was something that could make our surroundings a bit nicer, we embraced it. Having something beautiful to look at made such a difference. Of course, this was extremely risky for Tine to have done, and for us too – if they caught any of us, we'd have been punished in the bunker, or worse.

You had to protect your spoon, mug and plate with your life. Without them, you couldn't drink that foul soup or the nasty coffee. Theft wasn't as prevalent in the Siemens camp, probably because it was much smaller, but it did still happen if you weren't careful. When I had that awful diarrhoea, I couldn't eat my slices of bread in the evening so I stuffed them under my mattress at the head of my bed. I was woken up in the middle of the night by a hand snatching my bread.

The woman who had pinched it scarpered to the bed opposite and climbed in. I was surprised, especially because she'd always seemed like such a nice woman. Before being imprisoned she'd been a lawyer in the Netherlands. I simply let it go – I didn't want her to be punished and wouldn't have been able to prove it had been her anyway. It was very sad. Her mental health had been deteriorating for a while, and not long after this incident she was taken to the base camp, where she was most probably murdered.

She wasn't alone in her struggle. Some of the women were clearly losing their minds. Their change in behaviour would start with a strange smile, then they would start laughing loudly in a particularly bizarre way, and it would just get worse and worse.

I had a strong feeling that I wanted to survive – it's an instinct that is part of my character and has been with me my entire life – but for that to happen I knew you had to have hope. If you gave up hope you could sink into a depression and your chances of survival would disappear. I could see that that's what had happened to those women who lost their minds – they'd given up hope.

Most of the time I didn't think, I just lived. I was able to remove the bad thoughts in my mind, and that meant I could live for the moment. I also learned another valuable lesson, and after that I always ate my slice of bread as soon as I got it.

*

One night, the head *Aufseherin* was on inspection duty when she found me asleep on a camp bed in the back office in the Siemens barracks, even though I was meant to be on the night shift. Herr Seefeld had told me to go and lie down because I was so sick and weak. 'Don't go through that pipe, Van der Kuit,' he had said. By 'that pipe', he meant the crematorium.

The head *Aufseherin* was furious that I was sleeping there and our own *Aufseherin* was given a firm telling-off. She, in turn, shouted at me. It was the first time she'd ever done this. She must have been frightened to death that she would end up in trouble herself.

I was surprised that there weren't any other consequences. I had expected to be punished or beaten, but I suspect that Herr Seefeld spoke to the head *Aufseherin* and she decided it didn't make sense to report it to her superiors – in all likelihood she herself would have got into trouble for letting it happen.

At Siemens we were initially given an extra slice of bread at midnight, and once or twice we got a slice of German sausage too. It was my responsibility to share it out among the women, and I had to slice it up very thinly. There were as many as two hundred and fifty of us and just one long sausage. However thinly I sliced it, there was never enough to go round. Some women didn't get any, myself included. I told the women who missed out that they'd be first in line for some the next time, but often there wasn't a next time – the SS ate the sausages themselves, just like the food packages from the Red Cross.

The only other Dutch woman in my barracks was always crying. She had been imprisoned because the Nazis were looking for her Jewish fiancé. She told me he'd fled to Switzerland, but after the war she admitted he'd actually been in hiding with her parents. She was terrified that he would be found, and that he and her parents would be sent to a concentration camp. She would sit at one of the long tables, soldering the small components, tears streaming down her face. One day, Herr Seefeld asked me to go and find out what was the matter. It was perhaps thanks to him that she was released a couple of months later and sent home via a number of other camps. After the war she married her Jewish fiancé.

Once she had left, Herr Seefeld said to me, 'If you are released, Van der Kuit, go to the Siemens head office and tell them I sent you. They will find a good job for you.'

You really have no idea, I thought. He might have been well meaning, but I hoped he wouldn't try to help me, because that would mean they would look at my papers again. I was safer in the camp.

Herr Seefeld really tried his hardest to be nice. When I told him about two women I knew – a mother and daughter who were being forced to do hard physical labour in the base camp – he said they should queue up the next morning and he would arrange work for them in his barracks. He stayed true to his word; however, his actions weren't enough to save them. They always drank water from the tap and he told me to warn them how dangerous it was. I knew very well how ill it would make them, and did my best to make them understand, but they simply carried on doing it and became incredibly unwell. Not long after, the mother died. The daughter became mentally ill and was sent back to the base camp, where she too died – or was murdered.

On another occasion Herr Seefeld told me to gather up all the Siemens women in groups of five because he wanted to pay them. Again, he might have thought he was acting with good intentions, but I was dismayed. I was used to representing the working women and was friendly with most of them. I was a sort of intermediary between Seefeld and the prisoners – it was my job to tell them things, and they looked up to me a little. So I told them not to accept payment – after all, we weren't offering our services as labourers voluntarily. I was against the principle of it, and most of the women agreed with me – we didn't want to do anything that might create the impression we had accepted our situation. We were prisoners and we had to make that clear.

Herr Seefeld asked me to stand behind his chair and read out the names and numbers of the women while he offered them vouchers for the 'shop'. Each time a woman approached the table I would shake my head and she would say, '*Nein*.'

One by one they refused to take the vouchers.

After a few of them had done that, Seefeld said, 'Van der Kuit, tell them they can use those vouchers to buy tasty food and other items in the shop.'

'We aren't employees,' I replied. 'We are being made to carry out forced labour. What's more, there isn't even a shop in our camp.'

He was astonished, but kept offering vouchers for the work that had been done. When he brought it up again later, I reiterated that it was forced labour.

He expressed his surprise again. 'But you all broke the law, didn't you? That's why you're being punished.'

Poor naive man. I had to choose my words carefully, but I responded by saying that we were occupied by an enemy country that had its own laws, and that many women, especially in the base camp, were starving and dying of illnesses. He looked unhappy but didn't bring up the subject again. I'd said my bit.

Vally Novotna, a wonderful Czech girl, sat beside me in the office. She had a beautiful Slavonic face and was incredibly bright. Before her imprisonment in Ravensbrück, she had spent four years carrying out forced labour in a salt mine. She was always well dressed, in warm pullovers, boots and a nice jacket I envied terribly.

The Czechs were very influential in the camp. Many of them, like some of the German and Austrian prisoners, had been able to secure privileged positions in the base camp and the Siemens camp, mainly in the kitchens and in the *Bekleidungskammer* – the stock rooms where the prisoners' original clothing and belongings were kept. They had arrived a long time before us, many of them straight after Hitler's invasion of Czechoslovakia in March 1939. They formed a close community and helped one another, something that was key to their survival.

Vally seemed very fond of me; I was lucky to have befriended her. One day, when the weather deteriorated rapidly and I got bitterly cold, Vally told me to go to a Czech woman who worked at the *Bekleidungskammer* and tell her that Vally was a friend of mine. I was afraid – because you always were – but the following Sunday I set out to find her. I mentioned Vally's name and told her I was Marga. She seemed to have been expecting me and gave me a really nice black padded jacket and a warm hat.

I was very skinny – a couple of months in the camp had seen to that – but while the jacket was small it fitted me perfectly and I felt relatively smart wearing it. It even had an inside pocket in which I kept Pa's fountain pen. Who might that jacket have belonged to? Probably a Jewish woman who had been murdered there or in another camp, or a Jewish girl. Most Jewish women were sent from Ravensbrück to Auschwitz. It was horrific to think about the fate of the previous owner, but at the same time it was a relief to have something warm to wear. You had to take whatever you could. That warm jacket was a source of pleasure to me for the rest of my time there. I wore it all day and I slept in it too.

When I was feeling particularly down and unwell one day, Vally came over with a slice of bread with finely chopped onions on it. It might not sound too appealing, but it was tastier than the most delicious cake I have ever eaten! She told me not to give up and to think of something nice. Her kindness made me feel a hundred times better. We supported each other. Community played such an important part in our survival. Our friends were our family.

A couple of months later, just before we were liberated, I received a food package from the Swedish Red Cross – the only one that ever reached me. Vally came to the opening in the wall of our barracks, where a window should have been, and I gave her some of its precious contents: bread with liver sausage, biscuits and chocolate. She told me that the Norwegian and Danish women had also received Red Cross packages before they were liberated, but I didn't believe her. We hadn't seen any women leave or heard any mention of it. But Vally insisted, saying it would be our turn next. I couldn't imagine that could really be true.

Rumours of a liberation persisted. Vally had told me the name of her brother in Prague – a Dr Novotni – and I tried to track him down several times after the war, but it was impossible to make contact with Czechoslovakia for years. I tried again via the International Ravensbrück Association, but again I didn't hear anything back. I often wondered what had happened to Vally and hoped she had survived. Of course, she didn't know my real name and I'd never told her my true story. But I passed on both my names to the Red Cross when I enquired after her.

In 2010 I gave a talk in Ravensbrück, where I spoke to a number of Czech women who were visiting the camp and asked them to find out what had happened to Vally. In 2015 I heard that she'd been taken to Sweden towards the end of April 1945 and later returned to Czechoslovakia. Perhaps she has died by now; after all, we are rather old.

Some Sundays, our only day off, the Dutch women were convened to do very hard physical work rebuilding the garden and house where the SS commandant of the Siemens camp lived. My Dutch friend Thea Boissevain later told me that she had to lug heavy rocks and other building materials around. I should have been there too, but again I'd been lucky and got off lightly. When the *Aufseherin* summoned us, I needed to go to the toilet. I asked for permission. 'Yes, Marga, but be quick about it,' she said.

When I got back, the women had already left. I had no idea where they had gone and I certainly wasn't going to go looking for them. So I went to the kitchen block and sat down among the Czech, Hungarian and Polish women. Once I knew how to get out of this heavy extra work, I made sure to pull the same stunt every time. Given that those of us who knew how to avoid the heavy work were constantly exhausted from malnourishment and sleep deprivation, I can't even begin to contemplate how those who did it must have felt.

Sundays were also when the barracks were cleaned. If we weren't ordered to work, we would have to stay outside for the entire day, and we would try our best to stand out of the wind. As well as my padded coat I'd been given some closed shoes, so I was better off than many, but it was still bitterly cold that winter. Some of the women became ill as a result and were taken to the main camp. They didn't ever come back.

As of early 1945, conditions in Ravensbrück deteriorated further. The Russians liberated the concentration camps in Eastern Europe and the desperate Nazis moved as many prisoners as they could to Germany. As a result, the SS commandant and thousands of prisoners from Auschwitz arrived in Ravensbrück. One evening in January 1945 we were on our way to the night shift in the Siemens factory when we came upon a long line of shabbily dressed women who looked incredibly hungry.

'Holland, Dutch, *Hollands, Niederlanden?*' I shouted.

I tried calling out in French and German too. No one replied. They looked Eastern European, starving, sick, grubby and exhausted. They must have been either walking or locked up in train carriages for days. There were hundreds of them. Ravensbrück was now so full that the women in the base camp slept five or six to a bed. Women sometimes came to sleep in our barracks at the Siemens factory for a night or two, including an English girl who told us she was married to a Frenchman and had been arrested in France because she was working for the resistance. But we never saw these women again once the war was over.

We often heard shots. There was a path near Uckermark youth camp where women were taken to be executed in what we called the passageway of death. Others were taken to the surrounding woods or were gassed. At that time, a gas chamber and furnaces had already been built, and another gas chamber was transported from Auschwitz and installed at Ravensbrück. We could smell the daily massacres. Other prisoners who worked there told us what went on, so we knew it was true. The desperate Germans wanted to leave behind as few witnesses as possible; they were still murdering women on 23 April 1945, when the Swedish Red Cross was already liberating prisoners.

One day in January 1945 we were lined up for roll call as usual when we were told that we should go and stand near another barracks. A selection was made. We thought we might be safe because we worked in the Siemens factory – they needed us to work – but we were still afraid. We were told that the older women were to be sent to another, special camp

164

where they wouldn't have to work. That was a lie, of course. We later heard that they were assembled in Uckermark and gassed.

I tried to follow Vally's advice and think nice thoughts, but it was difficult. So many of our friends were dead, and there were times when I thought I was going to die too. I also wondered what had happened to my family, but I didn't dare think about it too much in case I ended up talking in my sleep. I even wondered whether the Germans had found a way of working out what you were thinking. It might sound silly now, but we were so disturbed by everything that was going on that we were no longer able to think straight.

I tried reciting poetry to distract myself. There was an English poem by Thomas Hood that I had learned at school and loved: 'I remember, I remember, / The house where I was born, / The little window where the sun / Came peeping in at morn.'

I can still recite it from memory, and the emotions of home and family that it elicits were very important to me. It is actually a very sad poem, but I don't think I thought about that back then. I found comfort in its familiarity. There were also poems by Rainer Maria Rilke that I knew off by heart, and Dutch songs that I sung in my head to keep my brain active and my morale up. I stole some paper, wrote them down and hid them.

This wasn't too difficult to do because I worked with paper in the office. But it was dangerous. If I'd been caught, I would have been punished and probably sent to the bunker. Many of the women took risks to write and draw, which may sound stupid, but the human spirit needs such things to stay alive – and small acts of independence and resistance kept us going.

My youth helped me to survive, of course, as well as my attitude. I learned how to push my worry aside and hold things together. I wanted to survive, and so I did everything I could to make that happen. I did not want the Germans to have the satisfaction of killing me.

9

My Real Name: *The liberation*

On 14 April 1945, the Dutch and Belgian women from the Siemens camp were ordered to go and stand outside. It was a beautiful spring morning; the sun was breaking through and it was just starting to warm up, so being sent outside wasn't a punishment. I'd only experienced Ravensbrück in autumn and winter, so the prospect of warmer weather was a relief. However, we were also worried – anything that deviated from the normal routine scared us.

We waited in the sunshine for a couple of minutes before SS soldiers marched us to the base camp. We were heading towards Uckermark, where the older women had been taken and gassed about two months earlier. I thought it was now our turn, and the pale faces of my fellow prisoners revealed that they too believed our final hour had come. My heart was racing. Was I going to die now, having escaped death for so long?

We had heard that the Norwegian and Danish women had been liberated a few weeks earlier, but was that really the case? We had our doubts. Too many women had heard stories of freedom or of a better camp and better treatment – which turned out to be untrue. Fortunately we continued walking straight past Uckermark. My heart rate slowed down again.

We reached the base camp and stopped outside a barracks. What were we to think? Everyone was speculating. There were wild rumours that we were going to be liberated, but that seemed unlikely. It was best not to hold out too much hope. It would be unbearable if those rumours turned out to be untrue. However, the Belgian and Dutch women had just received a food package from the Red Cross for the first time, and that gave us an indication that something had changed.

We were all talking at once, discussing all sorts of scenarios and trying to keep up our morale. There had been reports that the Germans weren't faring well in the war, but that had actually made us even more frightened – they were still murdering women on a daily basis and we knew they didn't want to leave behind any survivors who might talk about all the atrocities once the war was over.

'They're going to kill us,' we said to each other. 'They won't want the world to know what happened here.' But we agreed that we must not be killed. Not now, after all we had gone through.

We had to stay in the base camp for nine days. Nothing happened. It was an awful time, and we lived in constant fear of being dragged outside and murdered. We thought this was the end and became resigned to our fate. After all, there wasn't anything we could do. We had to line up for roll call every morning and every evening for nine days, for no reason. We spent the rest of the time either hanging around or sleeping in the barracks.

On 23 April 1945, all the Dutch and Belgian women were told to stay outside after roll call. We went to the main street. We were definitely going to be executed now, we thought. I tried not to show how afraid I was, but I couldn't stop shaking and was struggling to breathe. The guard called out our numbers, which didn't take as long as it used to as there weren't a lot of us left – many had been murdered or had succumbed to illnesses, and some had been sent to other camps. After that we were ordered, as always, to walk through the entrance gate in rows of five.

There were probably about 190 of us altogether. I walked beside my friend Dit Kuyvenhoven. Were we on our way to the gas chamber? Had my luck run out after all? I forced myself to keep walking as courageously as possible and knew my comrades would do the same. We were told to wait outside the entrance gate. Time passed, yet we still didn't know what was going to happen. All of a sudden we saw an open-top sports car in the distance, heading in our direction. We held our breath.

To our great surprise, the car stopped when it reached us. Behind the wheel was a handsome young man. We were flabbergasted. He jumped out of the car and told us he was there to liberate us. He wasn't wearing a uniform. Then he introduced himself and said he was from Sweden. He told us that his friend, Count Folke Bernadotte, the vice president of the Swedish Red Cross, was sending buses to pick us up and take us to Sweden. This seemed strange to us. It was so unexpected that I hardly dared believe it, but he was actually telling the truth. We could barely contain our excitement. After all that time, the war finally seemed to be coming to an end and we were going to be liberated.

The Red Cross buses were known as 'white buses' because they were completely white except for a large red cross on the side – so they wouldn't be mistaken for military buses and bombed. We waited and waited, very much hoping that we'd see one of the vehicles in the distance. However, we were disappointed again: the Red Cross buses didn't come.

In the end we started to wonder whether it was ever going to happen. We talked to the Swedish man, who was very friendly, telling him about life in the camp. Everything was so remarkable that it didn't cross our minds that we could sit down; we stood there like that for hours. He gave us some chocolate and cigarettes, the first we had smoked since being imprisoned. He lit one for me and I asked him to tell me what was going on in the rest of Europe.

My *Aufseherin*, who was leaning out of the window of her sleeping quarters brushing her black leather boots, caught sight of me smoking and yelled at me to stop: '*Nicht rauchen, Marga!*'

The Swedish man said, 'Don't listen to her. She can't tell you what to do now.'

That was when I knew we were really free.

When evening fell and there was still no sign of the buses, the Swedish man said we should go and get some sleep at the base camp. What a terrible idea! We didn't want to set foot in there ever again. I was worried sick that our freedom would turn out to be an illusion and we would be imprisoned again.

We told him we were used to working twelve-hour night shifts with barely any sleep, and that we wanted to stay outside on this wonderful spring night with the glistening moon above us. He was surprised that we didn't mind standing outside all night long, but we laughed at his naivety; he didn't understand what we'd been through and what life was like in the camp.

I don't think he believed the stories we told him. They were too horrific for a normal person to comprehend. Red Cross workers had visited the camp, but they had seen only the barracks where privileged prisoners were kept. Of course, they didn't see our barracks, the gas chambers or the punishment bunker.

Most of us stayed outside, apart from the women who were unwell. The nurses took them back to the base camp, promising they would pick them up again the next day. For the rest of us, the night flew by and we talked about all sorts of things. We were happy just standing there. Fortunately it didn't rain; it was a lovely April night, and we enjoyed the fresh air and the smell of spring.

While we were chatting we came to the mutual decision not to talk about our chilling experiences, but instead to look ahead to the future, to rebuilding our lives and societies. Of course, our stories came out eventually – and rightly so – but our main intention was to return to a positive life and not to waste a single minute of it. Too much had already been taken away from us. We had to focus on what could be salvaged, and we were determined that the rest of our lives wouldn't be defined by the gruesome things we had seen and experienced.

In the morning, three military trucks with tarpaulin covers arrived. Some of us were allowed to get in, and we were told

171

that white Red Cross buses would come and pick up everyone else. I was incredibly lucky once again, because three days later, on 27 April, all women and children left behind who were still able to walk were ordered to leave the camp – in what later became known as a death march. Regardless of how weak they were, they were forced to walk for miles. The Germans wanted to destroy all evidence of the existence of the concentration camps, so they transported the prisoners away from the front and the Allies. Hundreds of people died of exhaustion. When the Russians entered Ravensbrück on 30 April, about three thousand critically ill prisoners were left.

I was desperate to sit beside the driver in the Red Cross truck – if you sat in the back, under the cover, you wouldn't get a view of freedom. One of the other women had the same idea and beat me to it. She already had her foot in the door beside the driver before I even had the chance. I was furious. There was no way I was going to give up the spot I'd set my heart on. I grabbed her and we started fighting. This may seem extreme; after all, it was just a seat in the truck . . . But only people who have suffered in prison can understand how desperate we were to see the natural beauty around us.

The driver put an end to our fight by promising to stop after a while so we could switch seats. The other woman agreed, so I let her get in. The scenery was indeed beautiful, although we could see it only by peeping through a slit in the back of the canopy. Fortunately I was on the end of the bench, close to the opening, so I could see more than most. It was so wonderful I could hardly believe my eyes.

After driving for a long time we stopped in a forest and got out. We were given bread rolls, biscuits and drinks: items we hadn't seen in months. Daffodils and crocuses were starting to appear, and the trees had new green leaves on them. There was a wonderful smell of fresh grass. Everything seemed so unbelievably beautiful. All we'd seen for a long time was the grey dirt and the dinginess of the camp. We were incredibly happy, but our ordeal wasn't over yet.

All of a sudden we heard planes and shots. Our first thought was that the Germans wanted to capture us again or bomb us, but we soon realized that the planes were British ones. Our fear turned into joy, but not for long. They were still trying to strike us; we later heard that the RAF fighter pilots thought our trucks were full of fleeing Germans. The Swedish trucks had red crosses on them like the white buses, but evidently the Germans also used Red Cross trucks to escape.

Our drivers ordered us to leave everything behind and get back in the trucks. I still wanted to sit on the promised seat beside the driver, but the other woman shoved me away again. Once more we fought over the seat, even while bombs were dropping around us. I was furious about how she had betrayed me.

My friend Dit, who was in the truck in front, screamed, 'Leave it, Marga! Come and sit here with me.'

She leaned out of the truck and pulled me inside. We sat together at the end of the bench, by the slit in the fabric. After a while she said, 'Marga, there's something in your hair.'

She removed whatever it was – it looked like part of an eye. I shuddered and looked away. I can no longer remember having heard the explosion, but a bomb had fallen on the truck behind us. The driver and the woman with whom I had fought were dead. I'd been furious at her, but she had saved my life without knowing it. Poor woman. Like me, she had desperately longed to see freedom, but she had paid the price for that with her life – while I had escaped death for the umpteenth time.

We were driven to Denmark, where kind women who had prepared a delicious meal were waiting for us. We were exhausted, but so grateful to be alive, especially when we heard that thirteen women had been killed in the bombing.

The dinner was delectable and we devoured the food like starving animals. Our stomachs were no longer used to eating such large quantities or such stodgy food, however, so most of us became terribly unwell. When more prisoners arrived, the Danes were asked not to make any food that was too heavy on the stomach. We were still grateful for the friendly reception. It had been such a long time since anyone had been kind to us, and we were delighted that the Danes were treating us so well.

After a brief stay in Denmark, we took a boat to Malmö in Sweden. It was a beautiful day, and when we arrived we were received by a group of prominent and smartly dressed Swedish men, including King Gustaf V. We felt terrible in our rags. We must have looked like waifs and strays with the few possessions we had left. Two of the women, Hetty Voûte and Annie Hendricks, carried a box which held Annie's baby boy inside. He was only a few months old. We stood on the quay for what felt like an eternity and listened to the welcome speeches. It was all very lovely, but the only thing we wanted was to have a wash and get some sleep.

We were finally taken to a big museum. Mattresses were laid out on the ground in one of the rooms. All of the exhibits, apart from the very large statues and animal skeletons, were covered with rugs. First of all, we were given a delightfully hot bath and the Swedish women scrubbed us down from top to toe. I can still remember just how incredible that felt. Then all our dirty clothes and belongings were taken away and burned.

I tried to tell the woman who took my belongings not to burn my father's fountain pen; it was my only reminder of him. But she couldn't understand me. She didn't speak Dutch, English or German and I didn't speak Swedish. She indicated that everything had to be burned. I tried to stop it, but it was too late – the fountain pen had already disappeared into the flames with all of the clothes. I knew the fire was necessary to destroy the lice, but I wept all the same. All of the risks I, and others, had taken to save the pen had been for nothing. It had been so very important to me – not only because I could write with it, but because it felt like having my father close to me.

Once we were clean we were taken to another room, with racks of beautiful new clothes in it. We were allowed to pick out some underwear, two dresses, a jacket and a pair of shoes. I chose a green paisley dress and a blue one with flowers, a poppy-red Windsmoor coat, and a pair of light-grey shoes made from salamander leather. It was such a joy to have new, clean things in wonderful colours. We were also given a case into which we could put the items we weren't wearing.

The next day we had to give our names to a member of the Dutch delegation who was sitting behind a table in another room. I gave the name Margareta van der Kuit. Once everyone was back on their mattress, either chatting or sleeping, I went up to the man again.

'Is the list of names going to the Netherlands?' I asked.

'No,' he said. 'The Netherlands is still occupied. It's going to London.'

'But the post doesn't go to England. We're still at war, the Netherlands is still occupied.'

'That's right. But this list is going via diplomatic post.' He looked at me inquisitively. 'Why are you so interested anyway?'

I hesitated for a moment and then blurted out, 'I'm not Margareta van der Kuit. My name is Selma. Selma Velleman.'

I couldn't believe I'd said my real name out loud after all that time. When was the last time I'd done that? I didn't know. And I also wasn't sure I'd done the right thing. You never knew. I was still petrified that it might be dangerous to reveal my Jewish identity. But if there was a chance my brother in England would get to see the list, I wanted him to know I was alive.

The man looked astonished, but didn't say a word. He picked up his pen, crossed out Margareta van der Kuit and replaced it with Selma Velleman.

In the afternoon we had a medical examination. When it was my turn, I asked the doctor if there was anything I could help him with. The other women spent the whole time relaxing on their mattresses. They said they'd worked hard enough. But I couldn't sit still. I still worried about whether I'd done the right thing by revealing my real name, and I wondered what had happened to Pa, Mams, Clara, Louis and David. I didn't want to think about it. I really wanted to help and to take my mind off things.

The next day we were taken to Skatås, a small camp near Gothenburg, where we were interned. After all, the war wasn't officially over yet. The camp was located in a valley on the edge of a large forest, and it was cordoned off with chicken wire, trees and flowers. There were about a hundred women there, in wooden barracks with bunk beds. About twelve women stayed in each barracks, which was a luxury compared with the overcrowding in Ravensbrück.

However, not all of my friends were there. Women who were sick were treated in the hospital, including Wil Westerweel and Annie Hendricks with her baby. Unfortunately, her son died of diphtheria not long afterwards. Annie didn't have enough milk to feed him and he didn't have any strength or immunity. Many women died not long after we arrived in Sweden. They had become too weak to recover from the malnourishment and serious maltreatment in Ravensbrück.

Life in the Swedish camp was good, though. There was a sauna, which was something completely new to most of us. It was incredible to feel the heat of the steam, and to see and hear the water being poured over the coals. I spent a great deal of time there. It was wonderful just to lie still and let the steam cleanse me. I couldn't believe I was finally clean. It had felt as if I would never be able to wash off the dirt and lice from the concentration camp. As soon as I felt a bit of an itch somewhere, I would think it was a louse, undress and try to find it.

The camp also had its own clinic. We could visit it whenever we needed to, although I can't remember ever going to the doctor. We had become so used to walking around with dysentery and going to work with a cold, cough, injuries and exhaustion that most of us didn't bother. That camp mentality stayed with us. Fortunately, I wasn't struggling with my bowels as much now that we were being fed properly.

The food was excellent. We were allowed as much bread as we wanted for breakfast, with cheese, fish and meat. Lunch was plentiful, with delicious soup and more fish. I've got a sweet tooth, so I particularly enjoyed the desserts. We ate until we couldn't eat any more, even though the Dutch consulate had warned the chefs not to give us food that was too filling after so many of us had been sick in Denmark. We were also given ten kronor every week as spending money, which we could use to buy chocolate and cosmetics in the camp shop. When the war was officially over we were given passes to leave the camp and we were able to spend our money in the town.

Some Swedish families, and lots of young men and boys, came to the mesh fence. The papers had published articles about the girls and women from the concentration camps, and people wanted to see what we looked like. Some women didn't go up to the fence because they said they felt as if they were animals in a zoo. But most families were friendly and brought us biscuits and chocolate, and I loved being able to communicate with people.

I even made friends with one of the girls who came to visit us. She was a couple of years younger than me and had learned English at school. Although my English wasn't what it had been, we spent a great deal of time chatting, and once we were allowed to go in and out of the camp she invited me to her house for dinner. Before that, some girls had already made a hole in the mesh so they could sneak out to the town or the forest with the Swedish boys who came and flirted with us.

The Swedes inundated us with gifts, sweets and kindness. I tried to dispel any negative thoughts and accepted everything they gave us, enjoying every day. I was alive. I loved being able to walk around freely in nature, listening to the birds and looking at the flowers. The spring sky was wonderful: blue with soft white clouds nearly every day. It was almost too beautiful to be true and felt as if we were on holiday. I didn't sleep very well and had awful nightmares, but I was surrounded by friends. None of them suspected who I really was, but that was about to change.

So many women had been brought to the internment camp that we didn't all fit in the dining room at once, so dinner took place in two sittings. One evening, I went with the second group at seven o'clock. A man got up on the stage and asked, 'Is there a Selma Velleman here?'

He'd asked the first group the same question, but no one had responded. I hesitated. There was complete silence in the room. Then I stood up and said, 'Yes, that's me.'

That was the end of my false identity.

'I have a telegram for you.'

My friends were astonished. Speechless, in fact. Not only because I was the first person to receive post – at that point the Netherlands was still occupied so no one could send or receive letters – but above all because they realized they had never known who I really was. They later told me how surprised they were that I had been able to keep my real name a secret for so long, but they were so kind to me – their response was one of pure kindness.

I opened the telegram there and then. It was from my brother David in London. The message read, 'Very pleased to hear you are still alive. Any news of Pa, Mams and Clara? Love, David.'

It was wonderful to know he was alive – it was always in the back of my mind that he might have been caught by the Germans or bombed in London, but I was so sad to read his enquiry after Pa, Mams and Clara. He obviously knew nothing of their fates either.

That night I cried and barely slept a wink.

On 5 May 1945 the Dutch ambassador and Dutch consul came to tell us that the war was over; we had been liberated. The Dutch flag was raised and we sang the Dutch national anthem. We celebrated in the dining room with chocolates, cakes, orange juice and lemonade.

Now we were completely free I started making plans for the future. One of my fellow prisoners, Bep van der Kieft, had taught English at a school in the Netherlands. I asked her if she could teach me some English – above all, conversation. I already knew that David was in London, but I received a letter from Louis telling me that he was based there too. The idea I'd had that David might see my name on the list had worked; now they both knew where I was. Both of them intended to stay in England. David was still engaged to Sadie, and Louis had married a woman called Ann in 1942. I hoped I could go to England too and wanted to be prepared. In the days that followed, Bep and I spoke English together, and I started to improve my grammar as well.

I didn't have a lot of time to practise, because soon afterwards the consul came to ask if Thea Boissevain and I wanted to go to Stockholm to help the consulate with administrative work for ex-prisoners who were about to arrive from other liberated concentration camps. They were expecting thousands of men and women. He knew we had worked as secretaries before we were imprisoned and thought the role would be perfect for us. Of course we agreed.

When I first arrived in Stockholm I lodged with a very nice Swedish woman and her Dutch husband. They had been living in the city since before the war and she was a member of the Swedish–Dutch Association. She gave me various things while I lived with them, including some blue-chequered material to make a dressing gown from. The amount of freedom I had was incomprehensible. I was living in a normal house instead of a camp, eating normal food and wearing normal clothes. What an extraordinary change!

The other Dutch women and children from Skatås later came to Stockholm too. Additional members of the Swedish–Dutch Association put them up in their homes. Dit Kuyvenhoven was among them; she stayed with a Dutch diplomat's family in a wonderful house by a lake. Dit and I were allowed to use the house, bicycles and boats to our hearts' content. We certainly made the most of it. We cycled down the beautiful paths and rowed to a nearby island where we went swimming.

In the meantime, I was working for the consulate. My job was to contact sick people in the hospital, find out what they needed and make lists of the requirements. These lists were then authorized and sent off. For the first time in years, I had a salary again. Greet and I were in touch again too, and I was also in contact with 'Aunt' Jo – Mams' friend in Amsterdam. They told me they'd been left with nothing. They had been struggling to get food or a decent pair of shoes for months. I used my salary to buy shoes and stockings, underwear, fabric, needles and thread, and real coffee and sugar for them.

The Dutch ambassador called me into his office one day and asked if I knew a certain captain from the navy. I said no. The ambassador told me he'd dropped in with an envelope full of money for me, but I wasn't allowed to accept it because I'd said I didn't know him. Louis later told me he'd asked the captain of a ship travelling to Sweden to give the money to me. If only he'd said so, I might have been able to accept it.

After a while, Thea Boissevain and I were transferred from our lodgings to a small hotel in Stockholm, where we shared a room. We got on really well; I was glad we could work and live together. Several other Dutch people were staying in the hotel too and we became friendly with them as well. One of them was an older Jewish woman. She'd been saved because her son, who was a captain in the Dutch army, had managed to arrange a small fishing boat to take her to Sweden in the midst of the war. People did exceptional things to survive. That woman had a sewing machine and helped me make a dressing gown out of the blue material I had been given. It was wonderful, with a long, flared skirt. I couldn't believe I had something so beautiful. I wore it in London for many years afterwards.

I went on various trips with my friends, often camping beside marvellous lakes. All I wanted was to have fun and forget about the war. And although I managed to enjoy life in Sweden, I could never get rid of a subconscious fear – I still didn't know what had happened to Pa, Mams and Clara. Even though I suspected they had been sent to a camp or somewhere worse, I tried to suppress such thoughts and held on to a glimmer of hope.

During that time I also met a German boy who was a Jewish refugee. He took me to the cinema and out dancing, and we spent the weekends in the countryside with a group of other young people. He asked me to marry him, but I didn't feel ready for that. My freedom was too precious to me and I intended to seize every opportunity that came my way.

Eventually, flights to the Netherlands started up again and it became my job to make lists of all the people who had been granted permission to return. Dit wanted to go home as soon as possible, so I put her name on the first list. Coert Reilinger was another individual allowed to go back. I knew him from my time in Haarlem, when I used to go to the resistance meetings at Frans Gerritsen's house, and I saw him again in Sweden. He was one of the German refugees who had joined the Westerweel Group.

We were thrilled to see each other. He told me how they had been busy setting up a resistance group in France after Bob and I were detained. They were arrested too, but the Nazis hadn't had time to murder everyone. Coert had been sent to a prison in Germany, from where he had been liberated. We spent hours walking around, reminiscing about how our lives had been and talking about what we were going to do with them now. He was one of the German Jews who had gone to the Netherlands before the war to learn about farming so that he could go and work in Israel, and he wanted to get back as soon as possible.

I put his name down on the first list too, and we agreed to meet up again when I was back in the Netherlands. However, we never saw each other again. When I got back, Dientje told me that Coert had died in a car crash not long after the war, and Paula Kaufman later told me she thought it hadn't been an accident. She suspected he had been murdered because he knew too much.

Not long after flights started up again, my friend Thea also returned to the Netherlands. In the meantime, I was busy making sure that many other people who desperately wanted to go home got a spot on a plane as soon as possible. I put my own name on the list for the last flight in August – my brother David had said he'd be in the Netherlands then.

I will never forget that flight. Like most ex-prisoners, I had never been on a plane before. When the pilot announced that we were flying over the Netherlands, I looked out the window excitedly and saw North Holland's green meadows, tiny cows and horses below me. It felt like a miracle. When the pilot said we'd be landing in Schiphol in ten minutes, all the passengers cheered, 'Hurray!'

I was finally on my way home. I was pleased, but also afraid and sorrowful. Amsterdam – and, indeed, the rest of the

Netherlands – was a chaotic place after the war. Lots of people we thought of as traitors were still in government office, and some of them held fascist beliefs. The Germans had left us with nothing – there were shortages of everything. There were no clothes to buy, and people were wearing wooden shoes. There were hardly any cars on the road and jobs were hard to come by. People were trying to pick themselves up, but with difficulty.

On top of that, I didn't have a home to return to, or a family. I still didn't know what had happened to my parents and Clara. I hoped I would find them again, and I tried to keep my spirits up, but my arrival at Amsterdam Central Station was a major disappointment. Most people had family to meet them, but there was no one there for me. I felt very lost, lonely, and suddenly very Jewish. It was as though I were a guest in my own country, nothing more.

I had written to Greet, but she'd heard that we'd be arriving at Amsterdam-Zuid Station, so was waiting for me there instead. The trams were no longer running, so people who weren't picked up were dropped off by horse and cart. I was the last person left and gave Greet's address: 44 Tweede Jan van der Heijdenstraat.

It felt very odd to be back on the street where Greet and I had met as children. It felt like a lifetime ago. I was completely alone, but Greet's family welcomed me warmly and I was extremely grateful to them for that. It was very kind of them to take me into their home. Not only did they have nothing, but Greet's father was seriously ill. The apartment was small, and Greet and I had to share an old-fashioned wall bed. But I had filled the case I'd been given in Sweden with shoes, stockings, socks, jumpers and food, so at least I brought some supplies with me. Greet later said that finally having something to eat and something warm to wear saved her father's life. He was already relatively old, but lived for a number of years after that. It was the least I could do. I will never forget their generosity. They were such kind people.

David arrived in Amsterdam that same evening. I can still picture him walking into Greet's family's apartment in his uniform. We flung our arms around each other. What a joy to be reunited! It was 31 August, Queen Wilhelmina's birthday. He and I went to what was once a very good, renowned restaurant on Kalverstraat to celebrate, but they didn't have much on offer.

One thing they did have was pigeon, so we ordered one each. What a disappointment! The birds were extremely small and dry, and consisted of not much more than a few bones that had been cooked for far too long. I couldn't even get my knife in. Instead, we ate soup followed by two portions of pudding with ice cream.

We exchanged stories and talked and talked. He couldn't believe what a horrific time I'd had and was surprised to hear I'd worked for the resistance. His little sister! It soon became clear that I'd seen a lot more action than he had. I don't think he fully understood what I'd been through. After all, at the time, people knew very little about the concentration camps or the resistance fighters and political prisoners held in them.

He didn't ask many questions, though. Nobody did. It's

possible that they didn't want to rake over difficult memories and cause me pain, but I think it was a lot for people to understand. In any case, I wasn't sure how much I wanted to talk about it either.

I remember he was very angry with Bob for letting me go on dangerous missions while I was still such a young woman. He couldn't comprehend that I had grown up – quickly – and was now a grown woman with real life experience. In his eyes I was still a child, a little sister he needed to look after.

We were also incredibly sad; neither of us knew what had happened to Pa, Mams and Clara, and Louis was still at sea. I didn't know when I'd see him again, but at least we each knew the other was safe.

I couldn't stay with the Brinkhuis family for very long. They were extremely poor, and feeding another person was a great expense. However, the support Greet gave me was invaluable. We heard on the grapevine about lists that contained the names of Jews who had been killed in concentration camps. Greet came with me to social services and we studied the lists together. We found the names of Mams and my sister: Femmetje Velleman-Spier and Clara Velleman.

Greet held me tight.

I returned to my nomadic existence and wondered where I should go next. My friend Dit was living with her parents in a big house in Maarssen, outside Utrecht, and she invited me to stay with them. The trains still weren't running, apart from freight trains, so I packed my big case and got on a bus.

Dit's family owned a fruit farm that specialized in black

grapes that were amazingly sweet. The family was prosperous, and they were very strict Christians. Her father read from the Bible every evening before dinner as we stood behind our chairs, and we prayed before and after our meals. The whole family went to church twice every Sunday.

Each morning her father would knock on our door; Dit and her siblings all had to get up and help pick grapes. I didn't have to help, but I enjoyed doing so. We had to remove the very small fruits from the vines so that the others would become big and juicy. They were delicious.

After a week I decided it was time to leave. I felt as if I was imposing, and I didn't want to abuse their hospitality. I had never felt so alone before. At least during the war I had been busy and had helped people, but now I didn't have a purpose. I dragged my heavy case behind me and found a bus that would take me to Leiden. Again, I returned to my past. The apartment where I'd lived with Antje and Mien was now a student house. Antje was still there, but it was being run by my cousin Zetty and a friend of hers – another Selma. Zetty's daughter, Evalientje, was still living with her foster parents at that time.

It was Bob and Dientje who had told me that Zetty was still alive. We had written to each other while I was in Sweden, so I knew that she would be there. That was how it worked: you heard on the grapevine who was still alive and where they were. Fortunately, Zetty and Antje had space for me to stay, even though quite a few students were already living there.

Upon my arrival, I saw that they were drinking tea from a wonderful Chinese teapot. I recognized it at once and did my best to suppress a laugh. During the war, my bedroom had been on the top floor, and because the bathroom was all the way downstairs I used the teapot as a toilet at night. 'You shouldn't use that pot for tea,' I said. But they replied that it was too late; they'd been using it for months. The boiling water must have sterilized it!

I hadn't been lodging with Zetty and Antje for long when news reached me that something awful had happened to Bob and Dientje. When the south of the Netherlands was liberated, two young men had gone to Amsterdam to shoot Bob for revealing the location of the resistance meeting in Weert. They went to the house where he and Dientje lived, and waved a gun around, but they were so hopelessly ill-prepared that they missed Bob and accidentally shot Dientje instead.

Dientje later explained how just before it had happened she had laughed and said to them, 'Don't be so daft!' She could see that they were just silly young men who didn't know what they were doing. She ended up paralysed from the waist down and had to spend the rest of her life in a wheelchair.

The boys ran away after shooting her. Bob called an ambulance and the police arrested the two culprits. The young men's testimonies exposed the story about the information that Bob had provided to the Germans. When the north of the Netherlands was liberated on 5 May 1945, Bob was arrested as a traitor and imprisoned in a concentration camp in Limburg. I went to see Dientje; she told me that the allegations were true. Until then I hadn't believed a word of it. But I couldn't just ditch Bob and was determined to visit him.

Zetty told me about a farmer who travelled to the south of

the country by horse and cart a couple of times a week. I arranged to go with him and he told me where I should wait for him at eight o'clock the next morning. While I was waiting, another traveller approached. It was – by incredible coincidence! – my cousin Klaartje van Frank, who had handed down clothes to me as a child.

Neither of us had known that the other was alive, and we embraced and cried with joy. She told me that she and her parents had gone into hiding in Limburg, and that she had met a Jewish American soldier after the war. They had got engaged and she was on her way to visit him that day. A couple of months later they got married and moved to New York, where she still lives today, aged well over one hundred!

When I arrived in Limburg, Bob was in a terrible state, which was hardly surprising. There had been so many real traitors – men and women who sided with the Nazis and had betrayed Jews and people in the resistance – and Bob was locked up in the same camp as them. He had to live and sleep alongside them, although they represented everything he despised and everything he had fought so hard against.

After Bob was arrested, a mob in Weert had driven him around in a cart with a board around his neck with the word 'traitor' emblazoned on it. This was the man who had put his life on the line to save numerous people. He'd saved my life by finding a hiding place for me in Leiden, and I'd also been spared because he had given information to the Germans – Jan and I would have been shot dead otherwise.

Bob looked dreadful. It was clear how much he was suffering as a result of the accusations. Dirk Kraayenhof de Leur, the brother of Jan – who was arrested at the same time as Bob and me – was visiting him the same day. He told me that Jan had died when the concentration camp he was in – Neuengamme – was liberated in 1945. The Allies had bombed the ship he and all the other former prisoners were on, thinking it was full of fleeing Germans.

Dirk and I travelled back home together after this sad visit. It was a difficult time. That's not to say I didn't also have positive experiences in the student house in Leiden. I became friendly with a young man who had lived in Indonesia during the war and had been in a Japanese prison camp. He'd caught malaria there and was still suffering from it. I loved talking to him. He studied anthropology and inspired me to go and study one day too.

There was another young man there called Arnold Cats, or Nol for short. We fell in love. He studied medicine in Leiden, was full of life and always making jokes. He was exactly what I needed. We had a wonderful time together.

However, the future remained uncertain and I realized I wanted more direction. In November, I received a letter from the Dutch Ministry of War, telling me to report to them so I could be flown to London. This opportunity had come about because David worked for the Ministry of Defence in London. It was the first I'd heard about it – David had organized it all, but hadn't told me anything. I had mixed feelings about it. My brothers were in England and I desperately wanted to be part of a family again, but at the same time I didn't want to leave Leiden because I had fallen in love. However, the letter was more or less an order, so I couldn't say no. The only thing I could do was promise Nol I would write to him.

10

Living Life: *London*

I arrived at the Dutch Ministry of War in The Hague on 14 November 1945. I was driven by car to the airport, where a sergeant met me and escorted me to a small military aircraft that flew me to Croydon. At that time, there weren't any civilian flights in England.

David was waiting for me when I arrived, along with the cultural attaché from the Dutch embassy and a young Dutch lieutenant called Angelique. It was her job to take care of me. First I had to visit the embassy's official doctor. He examined me and asked me various questions about my health. Then we drove to a room in West London that David had rented for me. David had to go back to work again after that, so I was left completely alone.

The landlady was very nice, but I couldn't understand everything she said. She showed me where the bathroom was. The one thing I longed for was to soak in the bath for hours, but when I did this the landlady got so worried that she called my brother – she thought I was never going to come back out again!

Louis and I were reunited a few days later, which was

joyous. The five of us went out for a meal: David and his fiancée, Sadie; Louis and his wife, Ann; and me. It was great to have my brothers back and to be together again, but I also felt lost. Louis and David had both built an existence for themselves in England; they had been able to keep living their lives. I, on the other hand, felt as if my own life had been put on hold and I had to start again from scratch, without Clara, Pa and Mams. I'd even had to leave love behind in the Netherlands.

I got a job as a secretary in the medical service – in the same building David worked in. Everyone was very nice; the soldiers and officers brought me cigarettes and other gifts. However, I wasn't particularly busy and soon got bored, especially as I'd had so much to do during the war. My only task was to make sure the medical files of the young men training to become officers were available if the doctor asked for them. After their training, the men were sent to Indonesia to fight a losing battle against the independence movement.

The files were kept in a big cabinet, which only the doctor and I could access. They probably thought they were doing me a favour by giving me an easy job, and that I was used to keeping files confidential thanks to my work during the war. But I needed to keep busy to stop myself from becoming depressed. I felt lonely, and what I had lost really started to sink in. I missed my home and I missed Pa, Mams and Clara. I was always on the verge of tears. I had to keep reminding myself, 'You're lucky to be alive and to be in London. Other girls would give anything to be in your shoes.'

However, there were times when all I could do was cry, and

I had trouble sleeping. We didn't know what had happened to Pa at that point, but knowing that Clara and Mams had been murdered was simply unbearable.

Winter came and went. My first spring in London arrived. In April 1946, an Easter dinner was held for the military personnel, which I attended as David's guest. I sat opposite a sergeant in the British army, Hugh Cameron. He was a German Jew who had fled to England before the war broke out, and was actually called Hans Kalman – he'd had to change his name because of his position. He worked as a German interpreter who tried to determine during interviews whether soldiers from the Netherlands or other European countries were really German enemy soldiers. His mother and older sister had stayed behind in Berlin and been murdered.

We had a lot in common and it was nice to talk to someone about my war experiences. The fact we'd both had to adopt new names to get through the war created a bond. I always called him by his real name: Hans. He loved joking around and my life seemed to have some lightness in it again. We started seeing each other, but it soon became clear that his jokes masked a profound sadness. He was in a dark place and I couldn't help him; I was in a dark place too. It wasn't good for me to be with him and I broke off the relationship after two years. We kept in touch and he became a good family friend – he was godfather to my nephews – but he spent the rest of his life plagued by depression.

It was around this time that we found out what had happened to Pa. The Red Cross had drawn up lists and our worst fears were confirmed: Pa had been murdered in Auschwitz in December 1942.

David was living near me at the time and would often drop in of an evening. On one occasion he knocked on my door at around midnight and heard me crying. He came to sit with me and said that everyone's parents die and that I couldn't carry on like this. That was true, but not everyone's parents die in such a manner.

People around me seemed to think it was best not to talk about everything that had happened. If they did talk about the war, it was about the bombing of London. That was terrible too, but no one understood what life had been like during the war in the Netherlands. Or in a concentration camp. Most people I lived or worked with had never experienced life in an occupied country and couldn't imagine the things I'd seen and been through. Stories about the concentration camps hadn't really appeared, and there weren't many photographs of them either. People only had a vague idea about what had gone on. No one asked questions, so I didn't bring it up. I thought it would be best if others didn't know about the atrocities I'd witnessed. After all, our task now was to create a new, peaceful world.

I struggled to stay positive during those first months in London and often felt depressed. I needed time to mourn what I had lost before I could start building a new life for myself. I continued to feel terribly alone.

I often wandered the streets. David had told me where you could go for a cheap meal and, after eating alone yet again one night, I walked through Soho. I was peering into a shop window full of very sexy underwear when a well-dressed man approached me. He asked all sorts of questions. Where did I come from? Where was I living? Then he said, 'You don't belong here. You ought to go home.'

He took me by the arm and walked me to Piccadilly Circus Underground station. When I mentioned it to David he told me that Soho was the red-light district. I'd never heard of it.

My life finally took a turn for the better. I meant what I'd said when my friends and I were waiting for the Red Cross buses outside the entrance gate to Ravensbrück: we wouldn't tell the world about the atrocities we'd experienced; instead, we would leave them behind and not waste another second of our precious lives.

One day, Angelique – the Dutch lieutenant whose job it was to look after me – asked if I'd like to go out dancing with her. I said yes. She took me with her to the Ministry of Defence club. I had a great time and it soon became a regular fixture. She would wear her best uniform and give me her everyday one. That was where I heard about the International Friendship Club, and I decided to go and take a look one evening. When I reported to reception I was told there was another Dutch girl who was also a member. 'If you wait until around seven o'clock, she'll be here.'

So I waited, and she came. We spent the whole evening together and became very good friends. She worked for the Dutch section of the BBC. A couple of months later, she told me over lunch that she had got a new job with the United Nations and suggested I take over her work at the BBC. I met the head of the Dutch section and got the job. The salary was quite a bit lower than what I was earning at the time, but I was thrilled at the prospect of working for *Radio Oranje*. I'd secretly listened to it during the war with Wil, my first boyfriend, on a rug in the attic in Leiden.

During the Second World War and up until 1954, the BBC's foreign channels were based in Bush House, a crescent-shaped building in central London. Journalists, writers and artists worked there. Many of them were refugees from all over Europe. There was a very English, polite and friendly atmosphere. Everyone was nice to each other. Lots of people ended up marrying colleagues.

Each section had a head of department, a number of journalists and office staff. The Dutch section had three rooms, with old-fashioned brown furniture. One room was for the heads of department, one was for the journalists, and the other was for us. Four or five of us were based in that room, each at our own desk, and we all worked shifts. We broadcast three times a day: in the morning, at lunchtime and late in the evening. Two of us had to be there at any one time. Apart from typing out and translating the scripts, I also made voice recordings in the studio whenever a young Dutch woman's voice was needed.

Just as I sat down at my desk on my first day at Bush House, a girl came in. 'You're Dutch, aren't you? And new here? Would you care to join me for a coffee in the canteen?' she asked.

I was pleasantly surprised. She introduced herself as Jane Monnickendam. We went for a drink together and she became a very good friend. We would play tennis together or go out. Her grandparents were Dutch and her parents regularly invited me to their home. Lotte Fleming, who worked for the Austrian section, often joined us too. Her father was a German Jewish refugee and her mother was also German, but not Jewish. They had fled just before the war broke out.

Lotte had two brothers, one of whom was called Peter, who was a photographer for Kodak. The three of them lived together in a wonderful big house, not far from their parents, and they had a maid who cooked for them and did the housework. Lotte was close friends with an Austrian journalist in her section, Fritz, whom she later married. She, Fritz, Peter and I often played tennis together at the BBC courts near Wimbledon. We would also go out together, and Fritz and I would stay over with the Flemings. We were in love: Lotte with Fritz and I with her brother Peter.

Peter and I spent several wonderful months together, but our relationship didn't last. On the final day of the Olympic Games in August 1948 we were all invited to a big party, where we drank wine and had a great deal of fun. At the end of the night, Peter and I were almost the last ones left, frolicking and kissing in the corner. He suddenly whispered in my ear, 'Tell me you're not a hundred per cent Jewish.'

I was astonished. I don't think he was anti-Semitic – after all, he was half Jewish on his father's side. Perhaps he might have thought that he wanted to build his life anew and didn't want Jewish children, but I was dismayed and disgusted by what he said.

'I certainly am,' I replied.

I stood up and went home. That was the end of our love affair. I was finished with him.

A few years later, my husband and I were at the theatre. When we stood up at the interval I noticed Peter in the seat behind me. I gave him half a smile, but otherwise ignored him.

Autumn arrived. I was busy at work, which I enjoyed greatly. I'd been in London for three years now. Although I still had periods of gloom, they didn't overcome me as often as before. I even got through the winter – the darkness, the cold, and my tummy problems, which persisted. I met other Dutch women who were working at the BBC and got to know our Flemish colleagues too. The Dutch and Flemish members of staff often drank coffee and ate meals together in the canteen. I noticed one of them, a Flemish journalist called Hugo, who was tall and handsome with blond curly hair. He always had a book under his arm.

On 7 June 1949, I was on my own eating lunch in the canteen when Hugo asked if he could join me. After a while, he told me he had two tickets for a film preview that afternoon and asked if I would like to go with him. This wasn't anything unusual. Journalists who wrote about art, theatre and film were always given two press tickets, and they often asked us to accompany them. I told him I was on an early shift and would be free at two o'clock.

Just then, an English journalist called Charles came and sat down with us. He also said he had two tickets for a film and wondered if I would like to go with him. It was the same film. I told him I'd already agreed to go with Hugo, but asked if he would like to join us. So the three of us ended up going together, with me sitting between the pair of them. The title of the film was *Marry Me*.

After the film, Hugo asked if I wanted to grab some dinner at a nearby restaurant. I agreed, but as we were about to leave, Charles asked the same thing. 'Hugo just asked me that,' I said, but invited him to come with us. He declined. Hugo and I went to a large Chinese restaurant. He ordered a bottle of wine and we raised a toast to a delicious meal.

'This is extra special for me,' I confided, 'because today's my birthday.'

I'd felt out of sorts all day. Dutch adults make a bigger deal out of their birthdays than English people do, even if it's not a special one. I was pleased to have received a few cards from friends and acquaintances in the Netherlands. Hugo made up for it by ordering champagne and congratulating me.

While we ate, we exchanged stories about our wartime experiences. Hugo was from an esteemed Flemish family; his father, who was a doctor, had founded the daily newspaper *De Standaard*. The Germans had taken hostage a dozen young people from prominent Catholic families to coerce their relatives into supporting them, Hugo included. The hostages were treated well and released again a short time later. However, Hugo then became involved in the Belgian resistance. He was arrested and warned that he wouldn't be released if it were to happen a second time.

He fled to France after that, crossed the country on foot, and arrived in Spain via the Pyrenees. Once there, he was imprisoned in the Spanish refugee camp Miranda de Ebro. He was released in January 1943, sick and exhausted, and flew to England. After spending a few months working as a freelance journalist, he ended up at the BBC. I reciprocated by telling him about my experiences. I couldn't tell him everything, because there were some things I just didn't talk about, but it felt good to be able to chat a bit about what I had been through. When we had finished our meal, Hugo took me home before walking back to his place, which was not far from mine.

It became a nice habit: Hugo would escort me home after work. He often visited me in the hostel where I was staying and we would sit in the lounge with my housemates. He would bring drinks and cake with him, and everyone loved him. Men were only allowed in the lounge, though, and had to leave again by ten o'clock. He would come back every night and put a poem in the letterbox, which I would read the next morning. I have a box full of those poems, written in Dutch or French.

It was the height of summer and the weather was glorious. The girls and I would go swimming at the Serpentine Lido in Hyde Park and Hugo would join us. We often went to the cinema, theatre or a restaurant, and he always took me home again afterwards. I never had to walk alone.

In the meantime, I was also taking night classes in English and anthropology at the polytechnic in Highgate, and I ended up studying sociology and anthropology at the London School of Economics. After that I qualified as a teacher and taught maths at various schools before ending up at Sacred Heart High School in Hammersmith, where I was asked to set up the sociology department.

My name changed once again in 1955, but this time for a happy reason. Hugo and I married on 15 November that year and I became a Van de Perre. But I was still Selma. I've always remained Selma. I wore a red knitted dress. Very bold for that time! We had a good life together. My wartime experiences took a back seat, but they were always there. Hugo told me that I sometimes talked or shouted out in my sleep, although I couldn't usually remember anything about it in the morning. During the war I had been so worried about revealing who I really was by talking in my sleep, but no one ever told me that I did it. Perhaps I subconsciously felt safe when I slept next to Hugo so I was able to work through my fears and experiences in my dreams. Being able to talk about them also helped. Little by little I told him everything, often when we were talking with friends. I didn't talk to him about what happened with the Austrian officer in the German army, though – I didn't feel he wanted to know about that.

The year after our wedding, when my period failed to show up, I didn't give it a second thought. My cycle had never been regular after my time in the concentration camp, and I still had issues with my bowels. What's more, doctors had always said it was unlikely that I'd be able to have any children. However, because I developed other symptoms I went for a check-up with the doctor and he told me I was pregnant. I could hardly believe it!

Our son Jocelin was born on 23 June 1957. We had a wonderful life, first of all the two of us, and then the three of us. Hugo perhaps wasn't perfect, but he was the perfect man for me. After him I never wanted to share my life with anyone else. Through his work I was invited to numerous parties and receptions, I went to countless film and theatre premières, visited exhibitions, travelled all over Britain, and I met a number of fascinating people, including Charlie Chaplin and the Dutch athlete Fanny Blankers-Koen when I attended the Olympic Games on behalf of the BBC. I was invited to Buckingham Palace and 10 Downing Street.

Hugo died on 28 August 1979, after barely a week's illness. He had a type of cancer that the doctors discovered too late. The Dutch and Belgian papers that Hugo wrote for asked if I wanted to take on some of his journalistic work. I did. I spent twenty years as a correspondent writing about art and cultural events for *AVRO/Televizier* in the Netherlands, and for Belgian newspapers and television. I've had a rich life, and although I am now ninety-eight I still play golf and bridge, take painting classes, and travel abroad to visit friends and family.

11

Remembering the Dead

Although I haven't let my wartime experiences dictate my life, it is inevitable that they continue to play an important role. After all the risks my colleagues in the resistance and I took, we had a strong bond and kept in touch. The war has had a lasting effect on all of our lives.

Seven or eight months after I arrived in England, Bob was put on trial for betrayal. I was summoned to testify and returned to the Netherlands. I gave my testimony along with Frans Gerritsen and Jan's brother, Dirk Kraayenhof de Leur. We all said how wonderful Bob was and talked about the incredible work he had carried out. To our great delight he was released, but unfortunately the story doesn't have a happy ending.

After Dientje was discharged from hospital, Bob stood by her for a long time to care for her, but their marriage didn't stand the test of time. Dientje was very resentful. She later told me that she had never forgiven Bob for betraying the people who were murdered in the convent and for the fact that her life was ruined. She was also resentful because the shooting had left her paralysed and unable to have children. The tentacles of the war reached out and strangled the love and commitment that these two people had shared.

Bob and I remained friends, and Dientje didn't want to see me for a long time because of that. After some years, I sent her a bouquet of flowers for her birthday and we made up. She sent me a lovely letter thanking me for the blooms and invited me to visit her when I was next in the Netherlands.

Bob eventually remarried and had two daughters. He visited me in England, and he and Hugo got along very well. Every time he was in London for work, he would visit us and the three of us would go out for a meal or to the theatre. He loved Jocelin too and came to Hugo's funeral. Dientje survived Bob and lived into her eighties, much longer than the doctors had predicted.

Some stories from other colleagues are more heartening. Paula Kaufman moved to Israel after the war and I went looking for her. She was an incredible woman. The last time I had seen her had been in Haarlem. After leaving the Netherlands in 1944, she had gone to live in an apartment in Paris that was used by members of the Dutch resistance. Born in Poland, she had lived in Vienna since her youth and spoke fluent German, which meant she was able to get a job as secretary to the director of the Gestapo's building department in the French capital. It gave her access to a lot of valuable information that she was able to pass on to the resistance, but in the end she was betrayed by people she had thought of as friends and ended up in Bergen-Belsen.

After the war she volunteered as a nurse – she really was a

woman of many talents – and travelled around the refugee camps in Europe looking for her mother. Incredibly, she found her – an extraordinary story of determination and survival instinct and luck.

I sometimes saw Antje Holthuis too. In 1982 I stayed at her place for a few days and we went on some long bike rides together. On one of these excursions she asked me what I remembered of our wartime experiences and we shared lots of memories. She wanted to write these down for her children because they had so many questions. After a long period of wanting to forget and look ahead, the time had come to remember and look back. She believed we had to tell our stories – to people outside our families and circles of friends too.

I also visited Mien Lubbe, but her story is more tragic. She had always had problems with her legs – even during our time in Leiden – and walked with a limp. It turned out she had bone cancer. Wim Storm recommended an amputation, but she refused that for many years. In 1946 Wim asked if I wanted to visit Mien in her room in Amsterdam-Zuid. I took her a big box of Droste chocolates, even though they were very difficult to get hold of in the shops. By then, both of Mien's legs must have been amputated and she spent all day in a chair. I really felt for her. She was meant to be getting prosthetic legs, but so many people had left the concentration camps sick and injured that the hospitals were overcrowded and there was a shortage of doctors. She had to wait a long time before she could finally get them.

These brave people will always be in my thoughts and in my heart. On 5 February 1985, Mien and Antje were both designated Righteous Among the Nations by Yad Vashem, the official memorial to the victims of the Holocaust set up by Israel in 1953. Greet Brinkhuis and her parents, Cornelia and Cornelis, were also honoured for offering me shelter, help and support. Greet remained a very precious friend until her death in 2003.

All of those people did extraordinary things to help me and other Jews. Whichever paths our lives took afterwards, that bond between us will never be broken. Although I was determined to look ahead and not let what the Nazis had done ruin my life, I always carried these people and my wartime experiences with me.

On 29 June 1983, on behalf of Queen Beatrix, the Dutch ambassador in London presented me with the Resistance Memorial Cross 1940–5, an award for resistance fighters during the Second World War. I am very proud of this honourable distinction and of my work during the resistance, but I will never forget that I was just one of many people who fought against the inhumanity and did everything they could to save as many people as possible.

My family are in my thoughts every day. Losing Pa, Mams and Clara is still the most shocking thing that ever happened to me. Knowing how they were murdered is worse still than everything I experienced in the war, including my time in Ravensbrück. Despite being able to lead a happy and fulfilled life with my loving husband and son, I have never recovered from that loss. There's a devastating hole inside me that will never heal.

I reconstruct what was inflicted on them in the most har-
rowing detail. I wonder whether Mams or Clara knew what
was happening: those two sweet, innocent people who never
hurt anyone. I wonder whether they held each other's hands
when they died, and I wonder if Pa thought of us in his final
seconds or if he was in too much of a panic to be able to think
anything at all. Taking away someone's right to a natural death
is truly inhumane. Even now, seventy-five years later, I lie
awake at night and say to myself, 'Selma, get some sleep. You
can't change what happened by thinking about it.'

Although I returned to Ravensbrück several times, I could
never bear the thought of going to Westerbork, Auschwitz or
Sobibor. Standing at the places where Pa, Mams and Clara
spent their final days before being murdered would be too
much for me.

I know that it happened, but I still struggle to comprehend
how far some people are willing to go to rob others of their
lives in the most monstrous ways. By taking part in commem-
orations and by talking about the Holocaust I have found a
way of dealing with this.

Every April I travel to Amsterdam for an annual ceremony
at the Museumsplein, where I lay flowers at the monument on
behalf of the Dutch Ravensbrück Committee to remember all
the brave women who were murdered. Then I spend a week in
Ravensbrück talking to newly qualified Dutch teachers so
they can pass those stories on to future generations. I find all
of this very moving. At the end of the week there is a ceremony at the monument there and we throw roses into the
lake – the Schwedtsee – which contains the ash of so many

women and children. The first time I went back – in 1995, fifty years after the liberation – it was very difficult. I hardly slept for nights on end. Now I am more used to it, but it will never be easy.

One year on a return trip, one of the school students had written a poem about the Germans' heavy boots, and I was asked to read it aloud. It took me back to that night before I decided Mams, Clara and I should go into hiding – when Clara and I lay in bed and listened to the Germans raiding our neighbours' apartment. It was an emotional experience and I found the words very difficult to read. But I got through it and was told I'd done it beautifully.

After Ravensbrück I always go back to Amsterdam's Dam Square for Remembrance Day on 4 May. I lay a wreath of white and red roses to honour the victims, as a survivor and representative of Ravensbrück concentration camp. That is always very emotional. We commemorate everyone who was murdered. On 4 May 2019, with Katinka Jesse, Bob's youngest daughter, I laid a wreath as Selma, a resistance fighter and Holocaust survivor.

We celebrate the liberation on 5 May.

I am one of the few Dutch Jewish survivors of the Second World War. This is the story of how I, a twenty-year-old Jewish woman, ended up in the resistance and was ultimately arrested and imprisoned as a non-Jew in the infamous Ravensbrück concentration camp, the only concentration camp exclusively for women.

In no other country in Western Europe was the persecution of Jews carried out so efficiently and the death toll so high as in the Netherlands. At least three-quarters of the Jewish population was murdered, including my father, mother, sister Clara, my grandma, aunts, uncles and cousins.

I was one of many Jews who fought against the Nazi regime, and my story is an example of what happened to thousands of Jews and non-Jews. In this personal account I have recorded the minor details of our lives, the sheer luck that saved some of us, and the atrocities that took the lives of so many people. It is a tribute to anyone who suffered or died, and a tribute to my courageous friends and colleagues in the resistance who risked their own lives in an attempt to save others. We were ordinary people plunged into extraordinary circumstances. This book serves as a testament to our fight against inhumanity. The atrocities of the Second World War and the courageous acts of the people who defied them must never be forgotten. I hope this book keeps their memory alive.

Epilogue

My friend Greet moved house in 1995. When packing up her stuff, she found a box under her bed. In it was a letter:

6 September 1944

Dear Gretchen,
I'm in a cattle wagon with twelve people, in Vught.
Probably headed for Sachsenhausen or Ravensbrück.
You keep your spirits up. I'll do the same, although I do
wish the end was in sight. I'll throw this note out of the
train through a crack in the wall. Bye, my darling.
Kisses, Marga

Greet had completely forgotten about the letter and I never thought to ask her about it either. So many extraordinary things were happening back then that it was easy to overlook a minor miracle like the arrival of this note. A kind man, perhaps the station master, had sent it to her. A sign of life from me, Selma.

Translators' Note

As translators from Dutch to English it is often impressed upon us that our job cannot be very important because Dutch speakers express themselves perfectly well in English. In this case we were initially perplexed as to why our help was needed at all, as we were presented with a Dutch book that stated that it had been translated from the English, by an author who was clearly highly articulate in both languages. Readers might therefore be interested to learn how the book came together.

Selma van de Perre wrote her memoir in English. The manuscript was subsequently picked up by Arend Hosman, publisher at Thomas Rap in the Netherlands, for translation into Dutch by Rebekka W. R. Bremmer. The Dutch translation was further fleshed out by editor Catharina Schilder. The success of this work in the Netherlands, captured in a sample English translation by Laura Vroomen, generated interest in a full English translation. Andrea Henry, Selma's editor at Transworld in the UK, commissioned our translation. She interviewed Selma for supplementary details, which were integrated into the text by Rebecca Wright. The resulting manuscript was then re-read by Laura Vroomen. Selma is perfectly capable of presenting her own story, and the circuitous nature of this book's route to publication should be taken not as a sign of any failing on her part but simply of the fact that all good books, by the time they reach publication, have been a team effort.

Nevertheless, while working on the translation of *My Name Is Selma*, we felt that our job was particularly important, because of the serious nature of the subject matter and the need to bring this story to readers. We believe its value lies in the personal nature of the account, and, in contrast to an extensive literature focusing on World War Two, in setting the impact of the Holocaust in the context of the long and full life of an individual. Selma's story reveals a strikingly humble attitude to her survival, in an account that demonstrates immense resilience and strength of character, making this a truly uplifting read. As translators we go over the texts we work on slowly and repeatedly, handing the work back and forth between us, so that it leaves a deep and lasting impression. There is a great deal of sadness in this book, which could have made it a heavy task, yet Selma's inspiring attitude to life has made working on it an immense honour.

SELMA VAN DE PERRE (b. 1922) was a member of the Dutch Resistance organization TD Group during the Second World War. Shortly after the war she moved to London, where she worked for the BBC and met her future husband, the Belgian journalist Hugo van de Perre. For a number of years she also worked as foreign correspondent for a Dutch television station. In 1983 Selma van de Perre received the Dutch Resistance Memorial Cross. She lives in London and has a son.